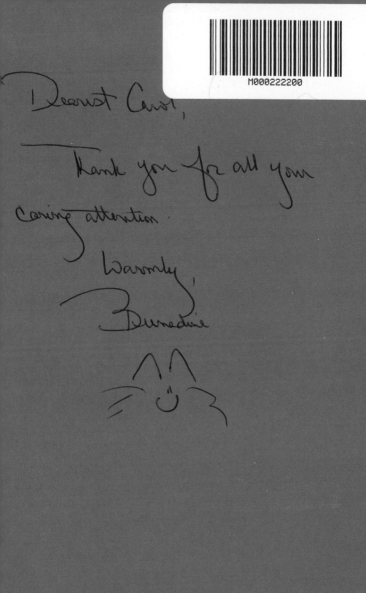

Dearest Carol,

Thank you for all your
caring attention.

Warmly,

Bernadine

THE
SECRET
SEX LIFE
OF
DOGS AND CATS

THE
SECRET
SEX LIFE
OF
DOGS AND CATS

BERNADINE CRUZ, DVM
ILLUSTRATIONS BY STUART RAPEPORT

The Secret Sex Life of Dogs and Cats
Copyright © 2005 by Bernadine Cruz, DVM

Illustrations by Stuart Rapeport, www.icandraw.net
Designed by Amy Inouye, www.futurestudio.com

First edition
10 9 8 7 6 5 4 3 2 1

ISBN 1-883318-52-1

Library of Congress Cataloging-in-Publication Data

Cruz, Bernadine D.
  The secret sex life of dogs and cats / by Bernadine Cruz.-- 1st ed.
    p. cm.
  Summary: "An almost-X-rated volume that's filled with all those questions
that you—and everyone else—were afraid to ask about your furry four-legged
friends. Nationally recognized veterinarian Dr. Bernadine Cruz explains the
secrets of every pet's personal life as well as setting the record straight on the
urban legends and lore of animal sex"—Provided by publisher.
  ISBN 1-883318-52-1 (hardcover : alk. paper)
  1. Dogs—Sexual behavior—Miscellanea. 2. Cats—Sexual behavior—
Miscellanea. I. Title.

  SF433.C78 2005
  636.7'0887—dc22

                              2005007945

Printed in the United States of America

ANGEL CITY PRESS
2118 Wilshire Boulevard #880
Santa Monica, California 90403
310.395.9982
www.angelcitypress.com

ANGEL CITY PRESS

To Howard, my very patient, loving
and supportive husband,
and to all my fur-covered friends
who have graced my life with unconditional love.

CONTENTS

INTRODUCTION

Warning: *This book is not for those hoping to learn about Labradors in leather or Abyssinians who are into S&M; however, it is rated "R" for risqué, racy and revealing. This book is not meant for children.*

SEX IS A TOPIC THAT MANY PEOPLE ARE STILL UNCOMFORTABLE discussing with their own doctor, much less their pet's veterinarian. It's awkward to admit you can't figure out if your kitten is Morris or Molly, puzzling to contemplate the difference between neutering and spaying (even though you think both are good ideas), and downright horrifying to realize that Buster's longest amorous relationship is with the neighbor's leg.

As a companion animal veterinarian for more than twenty years, I've met with many red-faced pet owners who don't know the first thing about his or her best friend's personal life. The misconceptions people have about pets' sex lives are funny, bizarre and occasionally tragic. When the owner of a young Siamese tomcat wanted to know if her cat's eyes would uncross once it was neutered, I knew I had to do something to lift the furry shroud of mystery surrounding the subject by writing an educational book about, well, pet sex.

Basic knowledge of the birds and the bees of cats and dogs is essential; the more you know about their reproductive physiology, the better you can understand their behavior. Also, there are major health issues to consider, for instance: most

9

owners are unaware of the fact that getting a female dog spayed before her first period (estrous cycle) decreases her chance of developing breast cancer by ninety-eight percent. Or that when an outdoor male cat is castrated, he is less likely to engage in dangerous activities such as roaming and fighting. And that neutering a cat subsequently reduces the likelihood of contracting feline immunodeficiency virus (FIV). These are things a pet caregiver needs to know, so you've picked up the right book.

The Secret Sex Life of Dogs and Cats provides the answers to all the burning questions pet owners were not afraid to ask—there's no inquiry too ridiculous or too weird to grace these pages. Most questions have been culled from my years of practice, and veterinary colleagues from across the United States submitted others to me when they heard I was working on this book. I try to avoid medical terminology as much as possible in my answers, but sometimes I can't help but talk "doctorese," so I've tried to define terms as often as possible without turning this into a veterinary textbook. And if you notice that I repeat myself, it's not that I'm absent-minded. In fact it's totally intentional. Some important points bear repeating.

Understanding how a pet's sexuality can affect his or her personality and impact long-term health will help you to better understand this important member of the family. Sex is fundamental; you wouldn't deny that about humans, so don't deny it in animals. But do keep in mind that a pet's proclivity to reproduce is not an emotional need like it is with humans—try not to compare the two. For animals, the need to reproduce is strictly a hormonally-driven phenomenon. When a pet is under the influence of these sexual chemicals, it will mate with unabashed abandon.

You can understand this desire when you realize that the words "estrous" and "estrus" come from the Greek word *oistros*—any thing that drives one mad, any vehement desire.

Unlike humans, cats and dogs can start reproducing when they are less than a year old, and continue producing litters throughout their lifetimes. A single litter of puppies may range in number from one to fourteen, with the average being eight. A dog may produce up to two litters per year. A cat's reproductive profile will allow a fertile feline to produce up to three litters a year. She can average four to six kittens a litter. In theory, a female cat and her offspring could produce more than 420,000 cats in several years and a dog and her pups could give rise to 67,000 new tail-waggers in the same period of time.

There just are not enough good homes and responsible, loving pet caregivers to accommodate these numbers. The problem of pet overpopulation is epidemic in the United States, condemning millions of absolutely healthy animals to destruction every year. With knowledge and action we can help solve the problem. If we love animals, we neuter and spay them, we give them food, a warm and fuzzy place to call home and all the loving attention they deserve.

CHAPTER 1

COURTING
THE BEAST WITHIN

BEGINNING WITH THE ONSET OF PUBERTY WE HUMANS LEARN to primp, preen, flirt, and approach the opposite sex with cautious determination. Our rites of passage are fairly predictable, but in the animal kingdom things are not always so clearly defined. What is instinctual to our pets may seem incestuous to us; some aspects of animal sexuality can be perplexing at best and, at worst, quite alarming to the uninformed. Who would have ever suspected that dogs could be into "golden showers" instead of engagement rings or that female dogs and cats resort to *eau de love* to attract the opposite sex? Even interspecies intimacies are possible. Once you appreciate the intricacies of wooing on the wild side you will see that in a broad sense, cats court and dogs "date" but these behaviors share little with human courting rituals. Please don't confuse them.

PET OWNER: *Can my unaltered five-month-old male kitten get my spayed adult dog pregnant by nursing on her?*

REPLY: Wow, this person helps confirm the need for this book. He must have slept through Sex Ed in high school. Though a cat and dog may be very good friends, they are different species—and separate species cannot reproduce (the exception, of course, is a horse and a donkey, which can produce a mule). Besides, this dog has been spayed, which means her reproductive plumbing has been removed—no ovaries means no eggs, no eggs mean nothing to fertilize. Therefore, no pregnancy is possible, even if this obliging bitch were to mate with a fully intact male dog, which is highly unlikely. In general, once dogs or cats are neutered, they don't mate because the hormones which dictate sexual behavior have been eliminated. Also, I hate to state the obvious, but no one ever got pregnant from nursing.

Aside from all of the above reasons why these two critters aren't able to produce any offspring together, here's another: when a male mammal is born, the testes are present but not functional. Although your kitten still has his testes, they won't produce sperm until puberty (puberty hits as early as six months of age). So even if your baby tomcat is having salacious thoughts about his wet nurse, at this point in time he is only shooting blanks.

Finally, if you're wondering where the milk is coming from in this scenario, your instincts are right: there isn't any. A spayed dog can't produce milk, and so this puss is doing the equivalent to sucking on a pacifier. Kittens will often suckle on another animal, a stuffed toy, wool clothing (it is theorized that wet wool smells more like mom than wet cotton or other fabrics), and sometimes even their owners, because suckling is a calming behavior.

PET OWNER: *My intact male dog always wants to sniff my crotch when I am on my period. Is he oversexed?*

REPLY: When a female dog is having her period she releases an alluring scent called a pheromone. When a human female is menstruating the smell of blood may be mildly similar to the canine sex pheromone and faintly stimulating to an intact male dog.

PET OWNER: *My pet rabbit keeps running around the house humping my cat. I don't want my cat to get pregnant—can that happen?*

REPLY: No, your rabbit won't be a father any time soon—at least

15

not of any kittens. This rabbit may not be randy; it's more likely he's declaring dominance. The act of humping is not always sexually motivated. Cats, dogs and even rabbits attempt to prove superiority through pelvic gyrations—it doesn't matter if they are intact or neutered.

A DISTRAUGHT WOMAN CALLS THE HOSPITAL. SHE HAS AN INTACT female Dalmatian and several other unaltered male dogs. She's just brought home a new male Dalmatian who has not been neutered. He immediately went up to the female and christened her with a "golden shower." What is going on?

Living with a bunch of brothers can make it difficult to lay claim to anything, especially if you might want to "lay it" some time in the future. This boy was just trying to mark the girl as his own. Subtle? No. Effective? Yes. Certain behaviors such as this boy's peeing on his new gal pal are considered sexually dimorphic, that is, attributed more to one sex than another. Aside from urine marking, other examples of male-associated conduct include roaming and mounting. The sooner a male is neutered, the greater the chance that these actions will be eliminated or greatly diminished. If a male is castrated later in life, these behaviors tend to become hard-wired in their brains (learned behaviors) and will persist post surgery.

Another frantic woman calls the hospital; she is crying pitifully. Earlier, her indoor cat escaped, but now the cat is back. But the female cat is acting odd, rolling on the floor and barely able to stand for more than a few minutes at a time. "Was she hit by a car?" the woman asks.

While it's true that this kitty is suffering, it's more psychological rather than physical pain she's experiencing. A car didn't hit the cat; she's in the throes of sexual frustration (that's right, she's horny!). The cat and her owner are experiencing the feline estrous cycle, the time when cat fancy turns to tomcat foolery. Female dogs have a bloody show that demonstrates to the world when they are sexually inclined. Female cats are not as overt. Cats do not have a "period." Instead they will announce their sexual urge by bending their bodies into a characteristic position: bum in the air, tail hiked to the side and crouched down on their front legs (a position called lordosis). Cats are often viewed as being aloof; however, at times like this they are extremely appreciative of any attention.

ALONG THE SAME LINES: MY NINE O'CLOCK APPOINTMENT IS A decorous woman who says her cat is "having seizures." The cat appears totally normal and I absentmindedly stroke the kitty's coat. As I run my hands over the cat's back and approach the animal's tail, she stops purring and extends her rump into the air. The cat's rear legs start pumping up and down in place and the owner freaks out, "See! She's having another seizure! What's wrong with her?"

Nothing is wrong with this cat; she's simply in "heat." What we casually refer to as "heat" is a combination of the proestrus and estrus phases, and is the time when cats and dogs are sexually attractive (proestrus) and willing to mate (estrus). If you find that your unaltered female cat begins treading with her rear legs, becomes extremely vocal or atypically amorous, she's simply got conjugal visitations from the neighborhood tom on her mind.

PET OWNER: *Are there whorehouses for dogs? My dog is getting pretty tense.*

REPLY: A bordello for Bowser would go broke. Though it may seem like male dogs mimic some men in their proclivity to have intimate relations with any willing female, the female dog only wants to fool around once or twice a year. Canine females are only sexually responsive during estrus (commonly called standing heat), a time when female hormones reign supreme. Usually, the canine estrous cycle occurs in spring and fall, although some breeds such as the Basenji only cycle once a year.

I EXPLAIN TO THE OWNER OF AN OUTDOOR TOMCAT THAT WE NEED TO test him for feline viral diseases, such as feline leukemia and feline immunodeficiency virus (FIV). The owner says, "Good idea. He is not fixed or anything, so I know he is not having safe sex. That's how they get FIV, right? Can I buy a cat condom?"

If you have ever tried to give a cat a pill, you are well aware that it can be a rigorous aerobic activity that often results in scratches and sweat. I don't think any feline worth his catnip would let a person attempt to affix a love glove to his member. Besides the fact that condoms for cats do not exist, FIV is not a sexually transmitted disease.

In the early 1980s researchers discovered a viral disease they termed feline immunodeficiency virus (FIV) in a San Francisco colony of cats. Though human immunodeficiency virus

(HIV) cannot cause illness in cats and FIV cannot cause disease in people, the two viruses are similar. (In fact, cats have been used as models for the study of HIV in humans.) Unlike its human counterpart, though, FIV is not sexually transmitted. Instead, cats typically contract the virus via deep bites that occur during fights. Though there is a vaccine available to help protect cats from this deadly malady, it is important for all cat owners to realize that vaccines do not afford one-hundred-percent protection. To safeguard your cat, keep him or her indoors and make sure he or she is neutered. Intact toms are most likely to get in fights, especially during mating season, and are at the highest risk of contracting the disease.

A YOUNG COUPLE BRINGS IN A FLUFFY, WHITE THREE-YEAR-OLD Maltese dog because of a bloody discharge "down there." I ask when the dog was last in heat. The blushing wife asks the perplexed husband, "Honey, has Bridget been running a fever?"

Bridget doesn't need a thermometer; the flames fanning her heat can only be extinguished by time or an intimate liaison.

CRAZY PET LAW:
A City in Colorado—
Cats may not run loose
without having been fitted
with taillights.

The dog's bloody discharge is called a bloody show, which signals that Bridgett's body has entered proestrus and is preparing to release eggs from her ovaries. The bloody show that a female dog exhibits during the estrous cycle comes from her uterus. Typically, the vagina will be swollen when a bitch is "in heat." Along with the bloody show, the bitch also broadcasts her sexual willingness during heat by releasing a special scent known as a pheromone. Undoubtedly, Bridgett is making all the intact male dogs in the neighborhood pretty hot with her *eau de love*; male dogs blocks away can detect this stimulating scent.

PET OWNER: *"How can my dog be pregnant? I only let her loose when she's on her period!"*

REPLY: If this owner was trying to use the doggy version of the "rhythm technique" they were totally out of step. They were letting their canine cavort at exactly the wrong time. The bloody show lasts approximately two to three weeks during the estrous cycle. It is during the second week of this cycle, called estrus or

CRAZY PET LAW:
A City in Oklahoma—
Dogs must have a permit signed
by the mayor in order to
congregate in groups of three
or more on private property.

standing heat, when she can become pregnant. Ovulation occurs on approximately the fourteenth day of her cycle. Canine eggs must mature in the uterus for seventy-two hours before they can be fertilized.

Though women and female dogs both have "periods," they are physiologically very different. A dog's bloody show occurs at the point when her body is preparing to release eggs and become pregnant. A woman menstruates when she has not become pregnant and her body is shedding the lining of the uterus that was built-up in anticipation of fertilization.

PET OWNER: *I only let my dog out during the day. How can she be pregnant?*

REPLY: I guess this person does not believe in "nooners" or early-morning trysts. A dog or cat that is under the influence of raging sexual hormones doesn't care what time of day it is.

PET OWNER: *My cat never gets out of the house. She can't be pregnant. She does live with an intact tom but he's her brother. They would never have sex, would they?*

REPLY: Dogs and cats are not above taking brotherly love literally. Incest is common. If you are an aroused Airedale or a passionate Persian, your sister is just as enticing as any centerfold in *Dog World* or *Cat Fancy.*

PET OWNER: *Can I breed my bitch back to her father? My breeder says it's fine and that he does it all the time.*

REPLY: Variety is the spice of life and mixing it up is essential for the prevention of genetic meltdown. Mating between closely related individuals is like having a slow leak in the cement pond—pretty soon you are left with a puddle of genetic misfits. Inbreeding can accentuate genetic defects that can have disastrous consequences, such as bleeding disorders, blindness and deafness.

AN EMERGENCY CALL COMES IN AT THREE IN THE MORNING. THE owner on the line is convinced that her Doberman has a hernia. When I ask whether it is a possible umbilical (belly button) or inguinal (groin) hernia, the owner says she did not know, "But wait a minute, it is going away!" Turns out the "hernia" was an erection.

Dogs will never need Viagra to get a '"boner" because a male dog has a bone in his penis that makes it constantly hard or erect. This bone, called the os penis, is cocooned within the fleshy tissue of the penis. (The urethra, which carries urine and sperm, runs over the top of the bone.) Most of the time all of this is enveloped in the sheath that holds the penis. So while the dog's penis is always hard, it's usually covered up by the sheath. However, if the dog is excited, licking himself clean, or involved in a bit of self-pleasuring (both intact and neutered dogs engage in masturbation) the penis extends out of the sheath and the pink penis is exposed. This is what the woman saw on her Doberman, and it's what any owner of a male dog, intact or neutered, is likely to see occasionally.

PET OWNER: *I think my dog is a sexual deviant. He is constantly humping his stuffed teddy bear.*

REPLY: This dog is likely masturbating. Numerous species in the animal kingdom engage in self-pleasuring—unlike some humans, they do not succumb to the stigma that this act is "taboo." In fact, masturbation is a normal, healthy act (for humans too). Pets masturbate for a variety of reasons: to scent mark, for stress relief, or simply for self-pleasure. They may also rub or groom their genital areas excessively in response to urinary or reproductive tract disorders. How can you tell whether your pet is just doing something that feels good or if she or he has a medical problem? Go see your veterinarian.

PET OWNER: *Can a dog's penis be removed? My dog has a habit of getting an erection whenever I come home. He gets really excited to see me, runs around the house for a few minutes, and then flops over onto his back with his bright pink penis, poking out of its sheath. He wants me to rub his belly but I refuse to have anything to do with him when he is acting in such a lewd manner.*

REPLY: Penises can be removed for extreme medical conditions, but the problem here is with the owner and not the dog. Obviously, this owner would have been happier with a female dog rather than a male, because the dog in question is simply exhibiting rather normal boy-dog behavior. He's excited to see his owner, and rolling over to show his tender underbelly is an innocent act of playful submission. Neutering may help curb some of his physical enthusiasm, but more likely, it will take training and time to extinguish this demonstration of affection. Try coming home and ignoring the dog during this overly exuberant show of affection—he will soon get the idea that his actions will not garner him the interactions he desires.

I ENTERED THE EXAM ROOM TO FIND A WOMAN SEATED ON THE BENCH holding a small throw pillow. She wanted me to identify the sticky material staining the fabric. She told me this was her recently neutered dog's favorite toy. Upon further questioning, she mentioned that he seemed healthy and well adjusted but would ride this pillow for minutes at a time with this silly glazed look in his eyes. "Is this pus from his wiener, or does he have a bladder infection?"

The offending substance on the pillow, presented as evidence much like Monica's Gap dress, could have been one of several different types of bodily fluids. Because this boy was recently neutered, he could be part of the eighty percent of dogs that can still ejaculate up to thirteen weeks post castration. Also, all male dogs, be they intact or neutered, have the ability to mount, masturbate and not ejaculate, so the fluid could have been urine or smegma, the sticky, stinky substance that lubricates the penis so it easily glides in and out of the sheath.

A LADY CALLED THE HOSPITAL HYSTERICAL BECAUSE HER SPAYED CAT just came in from outside and was acting "weird." She wanted to know if her cat had been raped.

Ever watch your veterinarian try to take your cat's temperature? Cats are very protective of that part of their anatomy. The chances of a spayed female cat being raped are slim. Unsolicited advances by any cat, dog, rabbit or person will garner the perpetrator a true appreciation of what a Ginsu master can do with ten sharp knives.

PET OWNER: *My neighbor runs a "stud service" for her Great Dane. What's that mean?*

REPLY: Your neighbor is simply pimping her pup (the "stud") out to other dog owners for mating with female dogs. A high-quality show dog can demand top dollar for sexual congress, and it's not unheard of for stud fees to be thousands of dollars. It used to be that dog owners would travel great distances to find the proper stud for their show dog, but today these purveyors of love can simply order "collected" semen from studs that is frozen and sent via overnight mail. Finding a reputable breeder, whether you are trying to find the perfect mate for your pooch or puss or a source from which to purchase your next furry addition to your family, requires that you do your homework. Just because a breeder states that its dog's or cat's lineage boasts champions and blue ribbons, don't immediately accept everything you hear. Does the breeder seem knowledgeable about the breed? Is the breeder aware of the breed's common genetic weaknesses and does the breeder screen for them when possible? Always ask for references and call them. Also query your veterinarian for suggestions.

A MALE CLIENT CALLS FOR AN APPOINTMENT FOR HIS DOG, COMPLAINing that the dog is "a girly man dog." The owner wants a "real man dog," and asks, "What can I do to make him more manly? He never lifts his leg to urinate!"

Some male dogs never learn leg levitation because they have led a sheltered life. Leg lifting seems to be a learned behavior, which is prompted by smelling the urine of another male dog or emulating a role model. I have known some male owners who were so troubled by the lack of limb lifting by their juvenile pups that they assumed the position of top dog and snuck out in the dead of night to personally demonstrate the finer points of raise and whiz in their backyard. Now, that is really trying to give your pup a leg up in life! Also, this owner needs to keep in mind that leg lifting is not just for male dogs—there are many female dogs that lift their legs, especially when they are urine-marking territory.

A CAT WAS PRESENTED IN THE EXAM ROOM FOR A POSSIBLE CASE OF rabies. Since our area is known to have rabid bats, I was worried that this kitty might have been hunting and eaten what he thought was a weird, flying rat. But when I examined the cat, he seemed to be in perfect health. The owner informed me that he brought the tomcat in after seeing him sniffing some of the shrubbery outside and curling his lips up in a sardonic smile for several seconds. The cat looked crazy, and the man feared the worst: rabies. The upset owner was almost positive that his beloved cat needed to be destroyed.

This story is an example of how much unnecessary drama can unfold when owners misread normal animal behavior. This cat didn't have rabies; instead, he was using a form of olfactory communication found in cats—and not dogs—called the

Flehmen or gape response. Felines possess a patch of nervous tissue known as a vomernasal organ in the roof of the mouth that allows them to "taste" a smell. This can be very useful when a tom is trying to locate a female cat that is in heat. The queen will release a pheromone in her urine. Urine is also used by toms to mark their territories, a warning for other Lotharios to stay away. It is likely that this cat was using his sense of smell to find out what other cats were in the area.

PET OWNER: *My dog has been humping my leg since I got his nails trimmed on Saturday. Do you think my groomer poisoned him?*

REPLY: One of the very earliest behaviors a litter of puppies will exhibit is that of mounting their litter mates followed by pelvic thrusting. These pups are not sexually precocious; they are establishing their places in the pack. When a dog humps a person's leg he is trying to show who the top dog is. How do you establish your spot as the alpha dog at home? Firmly and consistently push your dog off your leg when they attempt to mount and hump. Tell the dog, "No!" and ask him to sit and stay. There should only be one top dog in the pack and, if you are the dog's owner, that's you.

 **JUST THE FACTS**

The sexual habits and behaviors of cats and dogs often perplex their human caregivers. Our beloved critters do not care about our culturally variable morals when it comes to masturbation, simulating sex and getting-it-on. Unlike humans, cats and dogs are comfortable with their bodies, and normal bodily functions do not give them angst. If it feels good, they do it.

The female of both species is the governor of sexual relations. The female dog or "bitch" and female cat or "queen" dictate when (and where) they will accept the male for mating. Puberty is not heralded by the change in the timbre of a dog's bark or the pitch of a cat's meow; rather, it is when they are ready to mate. Canine puberty can vary tremendously from breed to breed and even within individual breeds, but it typically occurs when a dog is six months of age to a year old. Feline puberty is reached when a cat has reached approximately eighty percent of his or her adult weight. This coming of age can happen as early as five months of age, but normally happens before the cat is twelve months old. Purebred cats, the exception, tend to mature sexually at a slower rate than domestics.

A dog's reproductive cycle, called the estrous cycle, can be divided into four distinct stages that can be best monitored by hormonal changes. Sequentially, they are proestrus, estrus, diestrus and anestrus. Cats are considered polycyclic because if they do not become pregnant, experience a pseudopregnancy, or suffer illness, they will have recurring periods of sexual receptivity, separated by brief periods of resting (a short hormonal respite for a week or two called interestrus) during their breeding cycle.

Proestrus:

🐾 CANINE—Lasts about nine days. Signaled by swelling of the vulva and a bloody discharge (the bloody show). The discharge gives off a scent that is very attractive to male dogs and can be detected from miles away.

FELINE—Lasts only one or two days. No external signs. It is very hard to detect. A cat's vaginal tissue is not responsive to the estrogen surge of proestrus and thus does not exhibit vaginal swelling. She may become restless, show some interest in male cats but will not allow copulation.

Estrus:

CANINE—Lasts seven to nine days. Also known as standing heat, estrus is the time of ovulation. This is the only time the bitch will allow copulation, which results in the characteristic tie (see chapter 2 for additional information).

FELINE—Lasts five to ten days. This is a very vocal time. The queen adopts the characteristic bowing position that assists the male in mounting. Cats must experience sexual intercourse in order to release eggs from their ovaries (induced ovulation). A healthy cat that does not mate will experience a short period of hormonal quiet called interestrus. Interestrus lasts approximately fourteen days. During this time she will not be sexually attractive to toms and will not attempt to mate. Once interestrus has passed, she will resume all signs of estrus and again accept mating.

Diestrus:

CANINE—Lasts approximately fifty-eight days. If fertilization has occurred, hormonal changes prepare the body for whelping. It is also the time of possible pseudo pregnancy (false pregnancy), which is a self-limiting phase that persists for sixty days.

🐱 FELINE—This is a period of time that can only be detected by hormonal assays. If the cat ovulates, the site where the egg has ruptured from the ovary forms a corpora lutea. This region produces the hormone progesterone. If the cat does not become pregnant, the progesterone surge wanes with time.

Anestrus:

🐕 CANINE—Time of hormonal calm. Persists for about four months.

🐱 FELINE—Time of hormonal calm. It often starts in the fall and ends with the winter solstice and the lengthening days to follow.

Pregnancy:

Just as the duration of a pregnancy differs in humans, it can also vary in both dogs and cats.

🐕 CANINE—gestation usually lasts sixty-two to sixty-five days. Litters range from one to fourteen puppies. A dog may have one to two litters a year.

🐱 FELINE—gestation ranges from fifty-nine to seventy days. Litter size varies from two to six kittens. A queen may have two to three litters a year.

CHAPTER 2

THE INS AND OUTS
OF MATING

I HAVE VIVID MEMORIES OF THE TERROR I EXPERIENCED IN THIRD grade after my first kiss. It wasn't that my boyfriend was that bad of kisser (as a fourth-grader, he was, after all, an older man), but my conviction at the time was that I would get pregnant from this libidinous act. Granted, I hadn't even reached puberty, but that was a fact an adult would know—I was operating on sandbox logic.

It never ceases to amaze me that so many pet owners use a similar type of logic when it comes to their pet's sexuality—I call it "litterbox logic." The majority of us live in a society that no longer has ties to the farm. Even our command of the English language has been affected by our urbanization; ask a man to define the word "bitch" and he will mostly likely describe his ex-wife, not a female dog. (And I won't even get into all the permutations of "queen," which for the purpose of this book only means a female cat of breeding age.) But this lack of proximity to all creatures great and small shouldn't condemn us to abject naïveté when it comes to the pets who share our homes (and often even our beds). We grapple to understand why our cats want out at night, but I'm here to tell you, it's behavior that's perfectly normal. They're hoping to meet a partner and find a little lovin'.

The nocturnal sexual activity of dogs and cats has caused me to lose many hours of sleep. One night, I was working a shift at the emergency animal clinic and attempting to snag a short snooze. A technician with an urgent phone call soon interrupted my rest. I admit it: I was a bit miffed. I reminded her that it was standard protocol to recommend that all emergencies (perceived or real) should be brought into the clinic. Stifling a laugh, the technician told me the owner was physically unable to transport both dogs. My curiosity was piqued and I got on the phone. A man on the other end explained that apparently some neighborhood kids had snuck over in the night and Super-Glued the rear ends of his two dogs together. Or, as he put it, "I have a medical emergency—my dogs' butts are glued together!" Little did he know juvenile delinquents had nothing to do with his dogs getting stuck together—the pooches were just having sex!

Aside from keeping their human companions up at night, pets can also be an excellent form of birth control, especially for vets. Another late-night call set my cell phone ringing on the bedside table at home. I answered only to find a woman sobbing hysterically and apologizing on the end of the line. When I was able to finally calm her, she explained that her two Pomeranians were "locked together in love" in the backyard. What could she do? I recommended she just let nature take its course and give them some time. The dogs were "tied" together and this was a normal part of canine breeding. No, she said. She wanted them apart now. So I recommended that she spray them with water and hung up. Five minutes later, the phone rang again. She was even more upset. The dogs were still stuck. Now what? I told her to get some pots and pans and bang them together loudly. The noise might scare them apart. I turned over and attempted to go back to my previous activity. No such luck. The phone started ringing for the third time. Same woman, but this time she was no longer apologetic. She was livid. All my advice was not working. She demanded, "You are the vet. Do something!" I suggested that she hang up the phone and gently pick up both of the small dogs and bring them close by the phone. I would call her right back in a few minutes. "How is that going to stop my dogs from mating?" she asked quizzically. I told her that it was working for me!

PET OWNER: *Is it true that when dogs mate the in-and-out thrusting action causes a vacuum effect that sticks the dogs together until the suction slowly dissipates?*

REPLY: While the bonds of canine love are quite formidable, there's no vacuum seal to the action. Instead, during canine intercourse a phenomenon known as tying occurs. Tying is a locking mechanism that has evolved over the ages that helps insure that every last drop of sperm stays in the female's vagina. During dog sex, the male's penis swells as the muscles of the partner's vagina simultaneously contract, entrapping the male. The two dogs are stuck together for up to fifty minutes. (As many people can attest, all attempts to separate the lovers with blasts of water from a hose are in vain.)

The wheelbarrow position (or "doggie style" as it's more commonly known), where the male stands on his hind legs behind the female with his forepaws on her back can get tiresome, and being tied together gets tedious for the duo. It also limits both dogs' abilities to see what is going on behind them. Fortunately, the male canine is endowed with a flexible body that even Houdini would envy, and his penis is extremely pliable. Once the view from on top becomes boring, he swings his legs over the female's body. This repositioning results in the characteristic tail-to-tail orientation.

A CLIENT WHOSE MALE DOG I HAD NEUTERED A MONTH AGO IS IN MY

reception area raising a ruckus. He's livid, telling everyone in earshot that I'm a terrible surgeon and didn't fix his dog properly. Turns out his pooch that I neutered got his prize female pregnant, and he's so angry about it. He's going to get a lawyer and sue me. Wasn't it my fault for leaving some sperm behind?

Veterinarians do carry malpractice insurance and listening to this guy's rant, I started thinking about requesting a larger policy. After doing my best to calm the gentleman down, I asked him if the dog had sex with the female after she started having a bloody show. "Yes", he replied," but she had just started her period. It was too early for her to get pregnant."

For this pregnant bitch timing was everything. Though a bloody show is present at the start of the estrous cycle, the amount of discharge that a particular female dog will exhibit is extremely variable, and the amount of the show does not indicate the exact phase of estrous that the dog is experiencing. Some females keep themselves so fastidiously clean that their owners are not even aware of when the cycle begins, which could have easily been the case with this dog. It is also not unheard of for a female to allow a male to breed with her before she is in standing heat—the time of her cycle when she is ovulating. Because the canine vagina is the perfect biological incubator for canine sperm, the sperm inside could have remained robust for up to seven days. Possibly, the sperm just waited for the perfect moment to fertilize the soon-to-be-ovulated eggs.

PET OWNER: *Does the first time hurt for female dogs?*

REPLY: Fortunately for most female dogs and cats, vaginal tissue is very malleable and does not require a breaking-in period. But there are some cases that require assistance. Dogs have a hymen that can cause the virgin bitch to experience discomfort when mounted by the male. If a virgin female dog is bred by artificial insemination, her hymen is not ruptured until she whelps (gives birth).

A WOMAN THINKS THAT HER DOG MIGHT HAVE A TUMOR ON HIS PENIS. She explains to me that some days the mass grows even larger. When the dog enters the exam room, he happily rolls over for a belly scratch. I see a very normal looking, but engorged, head of a penis coming out of its sheath. Just to be sure I don't miss the reported growth, I don a pair of exam gloves and examine the organ. It's a perfectly normal dog erection. I pronounce the dog free of any foreign masses, but the owner is still upset. She can't believe his penis is supposed to look "so bumpy lumpy." And she wants one more question answered: "Why does he insist on sticking it out around me?"

Penile tumors are very rare. However, erections, for dogs, are not. In fact, male dogs (unlike human males) always have an erection due to the presence of the os penis, a small bone on the shaft of the penis. But male dogs aren't big exhibitionists, though they are always walking around with a hard-on, they discreetly keep it under wraps, encased in their penile sheath. A dog that is just happy to see you might pop its penis out of its sheath by contracting muscles that push the penis outward from its encasement.

A CLIENT REQUESTS A REFERRAL TO A BEHAVIORIST. I ASK WHY AND she confesses: her cat is a slut. The feline is so sexually promiscuous that the night before the owner watched her court several tomcats at once. To the owner's dismay, the cat mated with one male, then waited for a few minutes, only to do it all over again with a different tom. "She's got to be a floozy, because why else would she mate so many times?

This domesticated feline is exhibiting a behavior perfected by its distant genetic cousin, the African lion. It is not unusual for the dominant male lion of a pride to destroy the male offspring of all the females in his harem who were fathered by other males. Though this act seems barbaric, it helps to ensure that only his genetic material is passed on to future generations. Though our domesticated felines no longer live in prides, multiple mating helps to blur paternity boundaries and decreases the chances of infanticide by marauding males. There's another reason for repeated mating as well. Since cats are induced ovulators, one mating is often not enough to trigger the female to ovulate. Repeated matings will enhance the chances the queen will experience super fecundity.

PET OWNER: *When dogs do it "doggie-style" where does the penis go in?*

REPLY: When the act of copulation is properly performed, the penis enters the female dog's vagina. However, the male dog's aim may not always be perfect. When his aim is off, he may veer off her thigh, or poke her in the bum.

THE OWNER OF A VERY EXPENSIVE SHOW DOG IS BESIDE HERSELF. It seems she had shipped her dog off to a breeder who accidentally allowed a stud of lesser pedigree to copulate with her dog. Now the woman is convinced that her dog's precious bloodline is ruined. "Won't all of her other litters be tainted with the blood from the unplanned suitor?"

Though a scoundrel lured this beauty queen away from her betrothed, her blood will remain pure. Paternity of all future litters would only involve the stud of that particular breeding. (Even forensic science has gone to the dogs. It is possible to do DNA testing on a litter of pups to determine paternity. The American Kennel Association recognizes this technology and will accept pups for certification that are from litters that had more than one stud.)

A CLIENT WITH A FEMALE GERMAN SHEPHERD CALLS ME ON THE phone. He is taking care of a friend's four-month-old puppy while the owners are on vacation. His German Shepherd is in heat, but his friend assured him that the pup is too young for sex. He has just come home and found the two dogs sleeping together in the Shepherd's bed. "Is this young gun going to get my dog knocked up?"

Winter-spring relationships are not unusual in the canine world, but it still is very unlikely that this salacious Shepherd took advantage of the innocent pup. Male dogs, as young as four months of age, do have the ability to engage in sexual relations with a willing female but tend to shoot only blanks at that age. The capacity to produce viable sperm does not occur until nine to ten months of age, when a male dog reaches puberty.

PET OWNER: *If a dog mates with two different males, can you predict which pups are from which stud by order in which they are born?*

REPLY: There's no last-sperm-in-first-puppies-out rule. While it is true that a single litter of puppies or kittens can have multiple sires (fathers), you cannot predict the birth order. The uterus of cats and dogs is extremely different than that of human women. Though a woman can give birth to triplets and more, they all develop within the confines of a single uterus. Dogs and cats, however, are designed to have litters, so the pups develop not in the body of the uterus (which in cats and dogs would be too small), but rather within two horns that extend from the uterus toward the ovaries. When there are multiple mates, sperm from the sires mix in the uterus and horns before fertilizing the eggs. The mixing of the sperm allows for mixed-up paternity and mixed-up birth order in a single litter of babies.

CRAZY PET LAW:
A City in South Carolina—
Bitches in heat shall be confined or concealed from view while such dogs are in heat or proud.

PET OWNER: *Is it possible for a cat to be raped? Mine escaped from the house when she was in heat and a neighbor's cat grabbed her by the neck and had his way with her. When I ran outside to save her, he quickly dismounted and she howled in pain. Then, she threw herself on the ground, writhing in agony. I think now I should take her to a pet psychologist so she won't harbor bad feelings about sex.*

REPLY: A male cat's penis has backward facing barbs located on its tip. Cats, unlike dogs, are induced ovulators, which means that it takes the vaginal stimulation to cause the female to release her eggs from the ovaries. The insertion of the penis into the vagina should provide enough incentive for egg release but the barbs serve as a fail-safe mechanism. When the tomcat dismounts, the barbs prickle the vagina causing some apparent discomfort. The writhing on the ground that the female exhibits after the tryst is not associated with pain. The same type of gyrations can be observed when a cat is given some good catnip. Besides, given a short respite, this frisky feline is ready to entertain her next suitor.

As for the issue of rape, we must take care not to place anthropomorphic labels on sexual acts that we observe in the animal kingdom. Though we may treat our pets like our children, they are animals and respond to innate instincts when it comes to sex.

PET OWNER: *I heard that there are birth control pills for dogs. I gave my dog some of mine, but she still got pregnant. Should I give her two a day instead of just one?*

REPLY: Sharing is a marvelous thing, but not with medications.

Never give a drug prescribed for you or another animal to your pet without checking with your veterinarian first. Many of the drugs that people take can have dire side effects in pets—in this case, puppies. The reproductive cycles of women and dogs are extremely different. Birth control pills do exist for dogs but they only postpone the estrus (heat). This medication, a synthetic progestin, is called megestrol acetate and works by delaying the start of a dog's reproductive cycle. However, megestrol acetate is not recommended for long-term use. Instead, the best type of birth control for pets is spaying or castration.

PET OWNER: *Where can I buy perfume to make my dog sexier? I am trying to breed her but when the owner of the stud brought him over to my house, all the male dog wanted to do was jump around and play with my dog's toys.*

REPLY: We shouldn't fault this boy for participating in a little foreplay—dogs will generally tease and play with each other before mounting occurs. If either dog is a virgin, timid, or has previously been reprimanded for demonstrating sexual interest in toys or people, they may never settle down to the job at hand. Characteristically, it is the female who controls copulation. By taking the female to the male, you can increase the odds that coitus will take place. If they still don't seem fond of each other, try another stud.

PET OWNER: *My breeder says inbreeding is fine and that he does it all the time, but will it lead to a litter of idiots?*

REPLY: The less-enlightened species in this instance is the homo

41

sapiens, the breeder. It not the pet's IQ that is at stake. Inbreeding does not lead to a decrease in a puppy or kitten's intelligence, but it can lead to an increased risk of concentrating genetic characteristics called recessive traits. Some recessive genes code for superficial traits like fur color, but others can produce life-threatening conditions such as von Willebrand disease, a bleeding disorder that is found in certain lines of Doberman Pinschers, as well as other breeds. If someone were to breed two Dobies that carried this recessive gene, even though the stud and the bitch did not have clinical signs, their offspring would be at a much greater risk of experiencing bleeding problems. In recent years, concerned breeders and scientists have compiled breed registries that track the prevalence of genetically transmitted diseases. A conscientious breeder should always strive to pass on only the best characteristics of their breed, as winnowing out genetically transmitted diseases is a win-win proposition for everyone.

A PET OWNER CALLS INQUIRING ABOUT THE LENGTH OF A CAT'S pregnancy. I tell him that it's anywhere from fifty-nine to seventy days. He replies, "Do you think it will it be longer or shorter than that? The father is a Teacup Poodle."

There's no Teacup kitty coming out of this unlikely alliance; in fact, there are no such things as "catoodles;" cats and dogs do not mate with each other and produce offspring. They are two different species. And if your cat has very soft fur and a slight bounce to his step, it is not a "cabunny" or a "cabbit," the impossible union of a cat and a bunny.

PET OWNER: *A dog breeder calls complaining that she has two dogs she wants to breed, but they aren't interested in each other. "If I bring them in," she asks, "can you just hold them together?"*

REPLY: What attracts one animal to another is a matter of personal taste. Certain characteristics that guarantee more robust offspring such as general size and good health can contribute to attraction. The other contributors to animal attraction are pheromones, unique scents that contribute to sex appeal. But the most common reason why two dogs won't come together is that the female is not in standing heat—she's not at the point in her estrous cycle when she is about to ovulate. More than likely, the female is not hormonally and behaviorally ready to mate.

Assisted matings can be performed by veterinary theriogenologists, who specialize in reproductive medicine. This act usually involves masturbating the male to collect sperm and then implanting the collected semen by artificial insemination.

PET OWNER: *Why are male dogs such hound dogs all the time?*

REPLY: Unlike the female canine that is only receptive during the estrus portion of her cycle, males don't have to deal with hormonal fluctuations—they are ready to perform anytime. This characteristic is to the male's advantage on a genetic basis, as a male can sow his seed and continue his lineage with any willing female. He's got no need to be choosy, and can have his way with the female and then move on to another willing female. Since it is the female who must expend her time and energy in birthing and raising the offspring, it is to her advantage not to raise her tail to every dog that comes her way. If the suitor does not exhibit the characteristics that she deems will insure a vigorous progeny, she can wait for something better. As Robin Williams once said about humans, "A man does not need a reason to have sex—just a place." Ditto for male dogs.

PET OWNER: *I heard that cats are in heat because of the daylight cycles. If I keep my kitty in a dark place for a week will it just stop?*

REPLY: Yes, it is possible to fiddle with a cat's "love lights," but don't treat your cat like a mushroom. If you don't want your cat to light up your life with yowls of passion, spay her. It was shown experimentally that a cat would go out of estrous if exposed to light for only eight hours a day for several weeks. But as soon as the cat saw the light of the real day, the estrous cycle resumed. Cats are polycyclic, which means that they will have numerous sexually receptive cycles during the year. These seasons take place when there are fourteen hours of constant light a day, and each episode lasts for five to ten days. Indoor cats who are exposed to a combination of natural and artificial light can have much more erratic cycles.

PET OWNER: *Is there Viagra for cats? My male cat jumps on my female and does a quick pelvic thrust and then jumps off in a matter of seconds. I don't think he can do anything in such a short amount of time.*

REPLY: Male cats are not much for foreplay. Instead, he mounts, ejaculates successfully and dismounts in a matter of seconds. A tomcat can extend the length of his breeding time up to ten minutes, but no one really understands why some tomcats take their time while others simply hump and run. However, rapid intercourse does serve a purpose in the bigger reproductive picture. Brief coitus frees a female to mate repeatedly during her sexually receptive time—the greater number of matings, the greater the number of kittens she can potentially produce. This is known as super fecundity.

PET OWNER: *How can my dog be pregnant? She went through 'the change of life' a couple of years ago.*

REPLY: A dog can continue to breed her entire life. She never experiences a true menopause, though her estrous cycle becomes covert due to decrease in the bloody show. Though a female may still be reproductively capable, after eight years of age the percentage of uncomplicated pregnancies drops dramatically. The feline biological clock will also continue to tick as long as food, shelter and other environmental factors are suitable for reproduction.

PET OWNER: *My cat is driving me crazy! She keeps going into heat, and while I want to breed her in the future, I don't want her pregnant right now. A friend told me that I can stick a cotton swab in her vagina and it will stop her from crying all night. Do I need to lube it first?*

REPLY: Unless this is a prize show cat, the best way to regain your sanity is to have your cat spayed. Though your cat may still respect you in the morning, human attempts to simulate feline intercourse can't fool Mother Nature for long. Masturbating your feminine feline is possible but not recommended. This imitation intimacy would cause the cat to ovulate. These eggs would never be fertilized and, in short order, her body would realize that it had been duped. Soon the hormonal howling would follow. If a cat owner is insistent in retaining a cat's reproductive organs and delaying motherhood, a better alternative than attempting to create a homemade kitty vibrator is a trip to the veterinarian. Vets can give the cat a hormone injection that delays the reproductive sequence for up to seven months. However, some side effects are possible, including diabetes mellitus (sugar diabetes).

A WOMAN CRIES AS SHE CLUTCHES HER THREE-POUND FEMALE Chihuahua to her chest. It seems that when she was giving the dog a bath in the kitchen sink yesterday, she saw bleeding from her "you who." Is she going to bleed to death?"

No, the dog is experiencing a perfectly natural part of puberty. Human prepubescent girls are warned that "the curse" or the "monthlies" will come when they least expect it. Puberty in dogs can occur any time from six to twenty-four months of age,

CRAZY PET LAW:
A City in Oregon—
It is against the law for animals to have sex within the city limits.

although smaller breeds of dogs tend to be precocious. A dog's cycle is divided in to four stages—proestrus, estrus, diestrus and anestrus. During proestrus the vulva swells and there is a small amount of bloody discharge from the vulva. This phase is often not seen by the owner because a dog may lick the material away, trying to keep herself clean. Male dogs may be attracted to her, but she is unwilling to "put out." This stage usually lasts about seven to nine days.

The second stage, estrus, lasts about a week as well. This is the period of ovulation and is marked by heavier discharge from the vulva and willingness by the female to mate. This is the only time that she can become pregnant. After estrus comes diestrus, and the light bloody show turns light yellow in color. Though a female may still be enticing to the male, she is no longer lubricious. This phase can last for months. Finally comes anestrus, when the female dog is hormonally quiet for three or so months, and her external appearance is unremarkable. Then the cycle begins all over again.

PET OWNER: *My breeder says that her cats are known for having "silent heats." Does this mean that I won't have to worry about her waking the neighbors when she is horny?*

REPLY: Your neighbors may bless you and your kitty for never allowing them the distinct pleasure of listening to tom cats serenading from their fence line, but don't bet on it. Silent heats are usually seen only in timid female cats that live in large feline breeding colonies know as catteries. These shrinking violets are low cat on the scratching post of life and conduct themselves with the greatest deportment, never attracting toms. These kitties will have all the hormonal changes associated with the estrous cycles of their more demonstrative counterparts but they just don't exhibit the behavioral trappings of a cat in search of love. Dogs can also have silent heats. These female dogs often have little vaginal swelling and discharge. If the dog has a lot of fur in the perineal region and she is fastidious with her grooming, the cycling might not even be noticed by the dog's owner. If there are no nearby intact (un-neutered) canine Casanovas, she won't even raise a whisker of the other dogs in the neighborhood.

MY RECEPTIONIST IS LAUGHING HYSTERICALLY. SHE HAS A MAN ON the phone who wants to know if there are porno films for dogs. He has a young male dog that is trying to mate with the female dog next door. The owner seems very embarrassed because his male is more interested in the female's front end rather than the business end. "Do male dogs like blow jobs?"

CRAZY PET LAW:
A City in California—
It is a crime for dogs to mate within five hundred yards of a church. Breaking this law is punishable by a fine of five hundred dollars and/or six months in prison.

While I was in veterinary school, a professor of animal behavior showed the class a video of dogs, cats, elephants, pigs and other critters "doing it." It was amazing what animals can do without the benefit of hands! For this dog, however, a video is not going to be of assistance. It is not unusual for an inexperienced male to mount a female from the wrong end. This is time for an older woman to take control. A multiparous female (one who has had a litter) can take the boy by the paw and show him how it is done.

THE CLIENT FIDGETS IN HIS CHAIR, HOLDING HIS MALE MINIATURE Pinscher close. The problem, he explains, is that he has tried to breed the dog several times but the dog wasn't interested. "Can't you just give him a testosterone injection to make him like girls?"

With dogs, libido is not just the ability to get an erection. Male dogs always have an erection thanks to the calcified tissue (know as the os penis) in their shaft. The problem for this dog is likely between his ears and not between his legs. Supplementing a male dog with androgens will not increase his libido; instead, such an injection could decrease his production of sperm.

JUST THE FACTS

What attracts one cat to another or what lures a dog to a particular pooch is as much a mystery as it is in the human courting arena. Scientists speculate that the brawnier male suitor represents prime genetic breeding stock to a female, but this isn't always the case. Sometimes, for reasons only the psyche will understand, it is the less robust male who wins the paw of the maiden and succeeds in propagating his line.

The elaborate mating rituals that are seen in birds and certain other animals such as bighorn sheep are not observed in our domesticated cats and dogs. Some species will bond for life and only mate with another when the first mate has died. The queen and bitch are less discerning. They will breed with several males during the same estrous cycle. This seemingly promiscuous behavior helps to ensure super fecundity and the genetic diversity of the litter.

A single act of canine copulation can last for an hour, whereas feline intromission may be measured in seconds. The almost comical appearance of two dogs literally stuck together post coitus is in stark contrast to the "rage" exhibited by the queen once the tom has dismounted.

Copulation:

CANINE—Dogs do it "doggie style" with the male mounting the female from behind. The insertion of the penis is achieved with energetic pelvic thrusting. The "tie" is accomplished by the simultaneous swelling of the bulbous glandis, which is adjacent to the penis, and the contraction of the vaginal muscles. The male ejaculates a sperm-rich fluid within eighty seconds of tying. After this initial ejaculation, the male dismounts but stays locked with the female. He turns around in such a manner that the two are positioned rump to rump. This acrobatic move twists the penis one hundred eighty degrees, which occludes the veins of the penis and helps to insure the shaft remains turgid. Additional seminal fluid is pumped into the female, pushing the sperm-rich fraction further into the uterus. They will stay locked until the penis loses its tumescence and the vaginal muscles relax.

FELINE—Cats don't do foreplay. Instead, the male quickly mounts the female and grasps the nape of her neck with his teeth. At the same time, the female paddles with her hind legs at an ever-increasing rate until the tom ejaculates. From entry to ejaculation, the total elapsed time is only ten seconds. Since the feline is an induced ovulator, the backward-facing barbs at the end of the male's penis stimulate the vagina and cause the female to cry out as the male dismounts. The queen displays a moment of "rage" when she strikes out at the male. The male will wait to attempt a subsequent mating until she stops rolling on the ground and briskly cleanses her vaginal area. A feline will mate several times during her receptive period. This helps to ensure that she will ovulate and reproduce. She may have multiple sires to her litter, thus decreasing the chances of infanticide by a marauding male (if she is a free-roaming queen).

CHAPTER 3

WHELPING IN WONDERLAND

HY PARENTS THINK THAT ALLOWING YOUNG CHILDREN TO observe a cat or dog whelp—give birth, also known as parturition—will enlighten human progeny is beyond me. Having been present at the birth of my two granddaughters and the C-section of a close friend, I can attest to the fact that there is absolutely no similarity in the birthing styles of women and pets. Labradors don't need Lamaze; pets don't demand epidurals, swear at the father(s) of their litters or, for that matter, even issue more than a whimper. While human mothers will often deliver by C-section, only occasionally do bitches and queens need assistance in delivering their young, and the percentage that needs medical intervention or Caesarean sections is relatively low.

The expectant human and pregnant pets are also discordant in their desires to share the birthing process with others. Some women mark the entrance of their child with a cinematic extravaganza; delivery rooms get turned into sound stages complete with lights, video cameras and family members wrestling with the medical staff to get the best vantage point to see the baby crowning. Often, the footage from such a production features human anatomy normally not seen on prime-time television. Pets, on the other paw, prefer a quiet nesting box away from prying eyes and exuberant spectators.

No matter where the blessed moment occurs or how many spectators are in attendance, a visit from the stork can fluster both people and pets. One night, as I was deep in my REM sleep, a client called with an emergency. Her dog was in labor with her first litter and the woman didn't understand where the puppies would come out. I asked if she had any children. Yes, she had three. I inquired whether or not her children were all vaginal births. Yes, they were. I explained that puppies would come out the same place. "But it is so small!" she said in astonishment. "So was yours," I responded as calmly as I could, "it stretches!"

One of my clients who is extremely religious swore her virgin dog was pregnant. The dog had mammary enlargement and was rooting around in her dog bed as though she were trying to nest. Though this was a pampered Poodle, whose manicured toes never strayed out of its yard and had no contact with any other dogs, the owner was adamant that her dog was pregnant. After my examination and some diagnostic testing, I determined she was experiencing a false pregnancy, pseudopregnancy. The owner didn't seem to grasp that this was a secular problem. Before she left she asked, "She was at my church's Blessing of the Animals a few months ago, couldn't it be divine intervention?"

Mysteries of nature abound and pseudopregnancies are one of them. False pregnancies develop in dogs when ovulation takes place but fertilization does not. When this happens, all the signs of a real pregnancy, up to and including labor, can occur. The first signs occur around six to ten weeks after estrus and include weight gain, mammary enlargement and milk production—all signs that mirror a real pregnancy. Even today, veterinary science does not fully understand the exact mechanisms that cause a false pregnancy. We do know that the hormone prolactin, which comes from the pituitary gland in the brain and stimulates milk production, is involved.

The biological reason for false pregnancy may have to do with the ancestral pack nature of dogs—if a bitch produced milk, even if she did not deliver a litter, she could nurse and care for other pups in the pack. Treatment for the condition is a tincture of time. If a pet has one false pregnancy, she is more apt to do it again. The best solution, of course, is to have her spayed. Interestingly, queens can also experience pseudocyesis (false pregnancy) for all of the same reasons as their canine sisters, but they rarely take it to the extent of lactation.

PET OWNER: *Doesn't letting my dog have a litter make her a better dog?*

REPLY: Are women who have babies better women? See how absurd this question is? What makes a dog a "better dog" is a caring owner and early behavioral training. (The No. 1 reason why dogs are relinquished to shelters by their owners is because of behavioral problems.) Giving birth doesn't add to the personality of a pet, it merely adds to pet overpopulation.

AN OWNER ASKS ME TO EXAMINE HIS FEMALE INTACT CAT. FOUR months ago he saw the cat mate, and just this morning saw a kitten protruding from the cat's rear end as the cat used the litter box. But then, the owner explains, the kitten disappeared. The cat's urine must have dissolved her offspring. "Could you please take an x-ray to see if there are any kittens left inside her?" the owner asks.

I will grant you that pussy piss can be very pungent, but its ability to dissolve a kitten is zilch! Besides, a typical feline pregnancy lasts only sixty-three to sixty-nine days, so there is no way a cat could be four months pregnant. What this person probably saw as he spied on his pet's bathroom activity was a protrusion of the rectum called a partial prolapse. The protrusion is a portion of the pink-colored colon coming through the anal opening due to weak intestinal muscles. Partial prolapses may occur when an animal strains to urinate or defecate. At first glance, this protrusion could have resembled a kitten, but it most certainly was not.

THE PHONE RINGS AT THE EMERGENCY CLINIC AND ON THE LINE IS A gentleman whose Rottweiler is giving birth. So far she has had six puppies and things are going well, but he wants to know when she is going to have the other two pups. It seems she's no longer pushing and the last pup was born two hours ago. I ask if the dog had been x-rayed or had an ultrasound that confirmed there were eight puppies. "No," he said, "Isn't she going to have eight puppies? She has eight nipples!"

Following the same logic, all women would give birth to twins. Need I say more?

PET OWNER: *My husband wanted us to breed our white Miniature Poodle. She used to have the cutest little pink nipples, but now that she is five weeks pregnant her nipples have started to change color and are getting bigger. Is there a skin-bleaching cream I can put on them to keep them pink? Or can I bind her belly to help keep her nipples small?*

REPLY: There are some women who regain their pre-pregnancy figure shortly after giving birth, and others who don't. The same is true for dogs. Factors such as the number of pups in her litter, how much milk she produces, and how long the pups are allowed to nurse can all impact the mother's figure. And any changes that do occur are simply a part of life—bleaching and binding are not options. If you want your dog to retain her centerfold assets, spay her before that first litter is ever conceived.

PET OWNER: *My female Husky got knocked up. I want her to have a litter but I don't know who the father is. Is there a morning-after pill or something I can give her so she won't be pregnant any longer?*

REPLY: There are medications that can be given to dogs to terminate a pregnancy, but the side effects can be very serious and none are guaranteed to be effective. Because of this, most veterinarians consider the use of these medications to be unethical. The other alternatives for an unplanned pregnancy are surgical abortion or adoption. And keep in mind, one of the cutest dogs I have ever seen was the result of an improbable pairing—the bitch was a fifty-pound Samoyed and a fifteen-pound Lhasa Apso was the stud. Now that takes some ingenuity and persistence!

A MAN BRINGS IN HIS PREGNANT GERMAN SHORTHAIRED POINTER for a "special" spay. He found her mating with a neighborhood stray, but the owner wants to breed her to a pedigreed Pointer during this same estrous cycle. He wants to know if he lets her mate with the pedigreed male, "Can't you just surgically remove the mixed-breed puppies after she becomes pregnant?"

I don't believe any veterinarian worth his or her license would ever contemplate performing such a procedure. Even if someone were willing, it would be impossible to tell which fetus was a mixed or pure breed by inspecting the uterus. Each pup is surrounded by placenta within the uterus, and it would be necessary to cut into both to perform such an operation. The stress from anesthesia and handling would most likely result in the spontaneous abortion of the entire litter.

A WOMAN COMES IN TO HAVE HER DOG EUTHANIZED. BESIDES HAVING a very nervous dog tethered to a leash, the woman has two young, boisterous children in tow. It is obvious that the dog has recently given birth. I ask her why she is having this apparently young, healthy dog put to sleep. She breaks down in tears. The bitch has just delivered her first litter of two puppies. They were both born alive. The woman had wanted her children to experience the miracle of birth, and had allowed the children to be present throughout the labor and delivery. Shortly after the pups were born, they left the mother and pups alone for a short period of time. When they returned, they discovered that the bitch had eaten both pups. When questioned whether or not this dog had ever shown vicious tendencies in the past, she replied, "No, but don't you think the pregnancy made her vicious and next she will turn on the children?"

Cannibalism is not uncommon in dogs; it does not mean that the dog is vicious. A bitch may consume one or more of her newborn offspring for several reasons: if the litter is delivered by C-section or if the bitch is inexperienced as a mother, she may be agitated by the pups' presence and simply not know what else to do. Also, pups that are weak and doing poorly increase the odds that the new mother will react in such a manner. To help decrease the chances of cannibalism during and after whelping, it is advised to give the new mother some privacy. If this is the bitch's first litter or if she has a history of dystocia (an abnormal labor or birth), having one or two quiet adults present nearby, if mom will allow it, is a good idea. After all of the puppies have been born, periodically checking on the brood is best.

Some terrier breeds need to be muzzled when they are with their pups, at least until the puppies are weaned. Unless closely supervised, these mothers may destroy the entire litter (clearly these dogs will never win the Mother-of-the-Year award). Not all terriers will react this way, but if you were planning on breeding your terrier bitch, it is advisable to observe her demeanor post whelping.

PET OWNER: *I found a cat in the parking lot at work. She was skinny and pregnant when I found her. I took her home and made her an inside cat, and she started looking great. She filled out and her coat became shiny. I didn't know how far along she was in her pregnancy at the time, but after three months, she never had the litter. What happened?*

REPLY: Spontaneous abortions can occur in cats and dogs for a variety of reasons. Viral disease such as feline leukemia, feline herpes, feline panleukopenia and feline infectious peritonitis can cause an entire litter of kittens to die internally and be absorbed by the body. Or perhaps the cat gave birth to stillborns, which she consumed while you were at work (this is a natural animal behavior). Whenever you adopt a pet, especially if he or she is a stray or from a shelter, please take the critter to the vet for a thorough physical examination before you bring the pet home, or shortly thereafter.

PET OWNER: *Why are there never any kittens at Christmas?*

REPLY: Cats come "into season" starting in February and this time of reproductive readiness can last until October. Nature has focused the cat's reproductive calendar around the availability of nutrition for their offspring—longer days meant warmer temperatures and a greater abundance of food. Though mealtime for our present-day pampered pusses no longer requires that they hunt any further than their food bowl, their ancestors' concerns over a ready source of sustenance affected genetic breeding patterns. Most present-day felines tend to concentrate their breeding activities in the early part of the year. With the length of a cat's gestation (pregnancy) being sixty-three to sixty-nine days, this leaves a paucity of kittens for holiday giving.

And next time you are tempted to give a living animal as a holiday present, try a stuffed toy version instead. Once the craziness of the holidays is over, the toy can be exchanged for the real thing if the recipient is ready to take on the responsibility of raising a real creature. Remember, when you give or receive a pet, it is for life—the pet's life.

A CLIENT HAD AN APPOINTMENT FOR ME TO "CHECK A TUMOR" ON

61

her dog. When I entered the examination room it was packed with a woman, her six children and a large Labrador. I asked where the tumor was located. She indicated that it was under the tail. When I examined the dog, I found a puppy wedged in the vagina. I told the woman that her dog was in labor and had a pup stuck in the birth canal. She was utterly dumbfounded and asked, "Is she pregnant? But how could this have happened?" I couldn't help myself and simply said "Doggie style!"

It is not unheard of for a woman to be admitted to an emergency room for severe abdominal cramping only to discover that she is in the last stages of delivery and she didn't even know she was pregnant. How can a woman not realize that she is pregnant? Good question! You would think that having no menstrual cycle, gaining weight and spilling out of one's undies would tip off any woman that something was amiss. But, alas, emergency room medics can attest to this all-too-common scenario.

So it's no big surprise that some people don't even realize a pet is pregnant. Canine gestation usually lasts sixty-two to sixty-five days. The bitch may not show any belly swelling until she is thirty-five to forty-two days into being with pup. An observant owner may notice nipple engorgement and a color change of her teats from pink to a darker brown color during the third or forth week of pregnancy. And much like their human counterparts, dogs can also experience morning sickness at this same time.

PET OWNER: *I want to know if my dog is pregnant. Can I use one of my home pregnancy kits on her?*

REPLY: There are early pregnancy tests for dogs but such examinations don't include peeing on a stick at home. Your veterinarian can take a sample of your dog's blood and run a quick analysis to determine whether your dog has a bun in the oven. The test is best run at day twenty-eight or longer after conception. Presently there are no such tests for cats. Usually, however, pregnancy can be determined in both cats and dogs by physical palpation—vets use their fingers to feel fetal structures.

A WOMAN CALLED AND SAID THAT HER DOG WAS PREGNANT WITH NO exposure to any other animal. "How could this have possibly happened?"

Is the dog really pregnant? A thorough history and physical exam by a veterinarian would help to rule in or out conditions such as simple obesity, ascites (fluid in the abdomen), or a uterus bloated with pus or mucous (a pyometra or mucometrea). Blood test, abdominal x-rays and/or ultrasounds can all be used to assist in the diagnosis of what is truly going on.

Another possibility could be that the dog had a small amount of bloody show during her estrous cycle and was extremely fastidious; licking away all evidence of her cycle. She could have been in heat without the owner even being aware of it. Then, the dog had a quickie with the pup next door (dogs don't always have an extended tie) and is now pregnant.

JUST THE FACTS

There are no birthing classes for pets; typically puppies and kittens enter this world with nary a whimper from the mother despite the fact that she may deliver two to twelve offspring in less than twenty-four hours. Often, the delivery room is an austere closet or garage.

Birthing (whelping or parturition):

CANINE—Within twenty-four hours of whelping, the mother's temperature drops from its normal range of 101 to 102.5 degrees Fahrenheit to 98 degrees or lower. The bitch also starts to prepare her bedding (unless she has been provided one by the owner). The first-time mother (known as a primigravida) will not have milk in her mammary glands until the time of the actual delivery. If she has had a previous litter (multigravida), there will be milk in her teats before this time.

Stage 1—The bitch becomes restless and starts pacing around the house. She may start pushing her blankets around in her bed or commence digging a hole in the backyard to act as a nest in which she will deliver the puppies. Some bitches have a diminished appetite at this time.

Stage 2—The water bag (placenta) appears at the vaginal opening as the bitch strains. The mother typically bites the bag. The first pup may take up to an hour to pass. A headfirst presentation is the most frequent, but a breach or bum-first entry into the

64

world is not abnormal. The umbilical cord is quickly severed by the bitch. Dystocia (abnormal labor) can be due to a uterus with weak contraction or a mismatch in fetal/pelvic sizing. Dystocia is most common in primigravida (the first-time mom), small breed dogs, and almost a guaranteed event with English Bulldogs.

Stage 3—As the mother rests between expulsions of pups, she will clean the most recently delivered pup as it starts to suckle. She will also cleanse her vulva and consume the fetal membrane (placenta) that is passed ten to fifteen minutes after the pup is born. The action of nursing induces uterine contractions by the release of additional hormones by the bitch's body. It is during this time that if the mother is disturbed, she may halt labor for a variable length of time.

Stage 4—Labor starts up again. The elapsed time between pups can range from thirty minutes to two hours. The majority of litters are born within twelve hours, even when very large litters are involved. Uteroverdin, a deep green vaginal discharge, may be present for up to one week after all pups are born.

FELINE—Cats also experience a drop in body temperature before they enter labor, although it is not as consistent as it is with dogs. The last seven days of gestation will find the queen seeking a place to deliver. She may either be excessively social with her owners or shy away from human contact.

Stage 1—The queen may seem anxious and fidgety.

Stage 2—As she lies on her side, the queen will begin to labor.

Most litters are born within twenty-four hours, with each kitten born in rapid succession and little resting for the mother in between births.

Stage 3—The birthing sac (placenta) is passed with the kittens and consumed by the queen. If queen is disturbed during the kittening process, she may stop laboring, relocate her kittens, and then recommence labor. As with the canine, a normal dark green-to-brown vaginal discharge (uteroverdin) will be present after the litter is born. This discharge should cease approximately twelve hours after the kittening. Difficulty with delivery is uncommon but may occur for the same reasons as with dogs.

CHAPTER 4

THE PATTER
OF
LITTLE PAWS

WHEN I PREPARED TO GO INTO MEDICINE, I HAD TO MAKE A decision to become a pediatrician or a veterinarian. I chose veterinarian, because I couldn't resist the thoughts of getting paid to snuggle newborn fuzzies and being slathered with kisses from golden retriever puppies with sour baby-milk breath. But even with my love of pups and kittens, I still passionately urge all my clients to spay and neuter their pets. Pet overpopulation is an epidemic: of the estimated sixty-five million cats and seventy-seven million dogs in the United States, more than a million pets are destroyed each year in animal control facilities throughout the United States because there are not enough good homes to go around.

One third of all feline and canine custodians consider their pets to be their children or, at least, family members. Parenthood, whether the object of your affection stands on two legs or four, is an awesome responsibility. Aside from the emotional connections, pets also come with financial liabilities (though, thankfully, you don't have to send the furry children to college). That free bundle of fur that was given away at the grocery store needs food and veterinary care, at the very minimum. The sad reality of pet acquisition without forethought is a strained human-animal bond. Medical or behavioral needs may not be met. When these bonds are broken it is usually the pet who suffers. Tragically, this worst-case scenario often ends up with the pet being destroyed.

Though pet parents think of their furry charges as their kids, pets are not humans and some of the techniques used in caring for our bipedal youngsters don't suit our quadrupeds. Though newborn kittens, puppies and human babies can all easily communicate their need for sustenance, there are very disparate techniques needed to care for each of these babies. Pop a baby bottle in a novice father's hands, and he will eventually figure out how to get the nipple into the baby's mouth and satiate the fruit of his loins. If you position a suckling puppy or kitten similarly on its back, however, he or she is likely to inhale the milk into his or her lungs and develop aspiration pneumonia, an often fatal condition. Faced with being a wet nurse to a canine or feline newborn, it is more appropriate to place the babe in the palm of your hand with its tummy next to your palm, its head facing towards your fingers. Gently raise its chin up to a forty-five-degree angle and then insert the pet nursing bottle nipple into proffered lips. Though we may love them the same, pets have special needs and can't be raised like human babies.

Ask a mother the best way to feed, burp or bathe her newborn baby and you will get as many different answers as there are grandmothers. Pet parents often find themselves in the same quandary when taking care of newborn critters—they are torn between what seems logical and what the breeder, a friend or someone on the Internet has to say. A quick word about breeders: for all intents and purposes, a dog is a dog and a cat is just a cat even if it comes complete with a blue-ribbon pedigree. Breeders often will have some very strong opinions regarding everything from what to feed their breed, what vaccines can and cannot be given, when these immunizations should be given and whether or not the animal should be neutered. These opinions are not always based on real science. When in doubt as to how best to care for your pet, ask your veterinarian. He or she is more likely to be current on recent advances in veterinary medicine and can evaluate the health needs of your particular pet. But before I raise the ire of breeders everywhere, I readily admit that there are some fantastic individuals in this group who are extremely devoted to their breeds and, through their efforts, have raised the standard of well-being for their charges. But enlightenment is not universal for them all, as can be seen from the following . . .

PET OWNER: *My breeder said that if puppies are born by Caesarean section, it is critically important to stimulate them before they will have their first bowel movement. Do I really have to insert a match into the puppies' rectums to get them to poop?*

REPLY: I hope the breeder remembers to blow it out first. Yes, it is necessary to stimulate a newborn puppy or kitten to defecate and urinate, but NO! you don't have to do it—this is a job that the bitch or queen tends to while grooming the newborns. If you have an orphaned puppy and need to play mom yourself, you do not need to lick the baby's bum. A warmed wet hand towel or baby wipes work very nicely. Using an unlit match does work and is a trick that many breeders will use on newborns, but I do NOT recommend doing this. There are better ways to do things. Around the time of weaning (when nursing stops), puppies and kittens have learned to handle the call of nature on their own.

PET OWNER: *My stud is a dud! I don't think my cat produces enough sperm. I have used him for breeding several times and with a different mate each time—and yet all of the litters have only*

*had two or three kittens. Is there anything I can do to increase his
sperm count?*

REPLY: Your tom is not a failure as a father, it is the mother
who determines litter size. Her fecundity is based on the number of times she copulates, her nutritional status and her general health. And take note, before a queen is bred, she should
be current on all vaccines, free from internal parasites and
test negative for the contagious feline viruses.

A WOMAN CALLS WHO IS TRYING TO TAKE CARE OF AN UNWEANED
orphan puppy. She knows that mother's milk is the best thing for
the young pup nutritionally. "I just had a baby myself, can I just
breast feed the pup on me?"

This is *not* what the human-animal bond means. Having a
close relationship with your pet is important, but not this close.
Plus, every species' milk varies tremendously in its protein and
fat composition. A mother rabbit, for instance, nurses her babies
only once a day due to the high content of fat in the milk. Human
milk is not the best choice for puppies or kittens because of the
difference in composition. However, there are several commer-
cially available milk replacements for these orphans. Canned
goat's milk, in particular, is a good alternative.

PET OWNER: *I have a male chauvinist cat. He refuses to help care
for his kittens once they are born. He loves playing with my female
before and after her pregnancies, but once the kittens come along
he wants nothing to do with the mother until all the kittens are out*

of the house. What can I do to increase his involvement in bring-
ing up baby?

REPLY: Free-living cats live in a matriarchal society, i.e. girls
rule, boys drool. The feral male lives in the colony until the
time of puberty, then he moves out to live a solitary life. We
have changed the dynamics of feline social order by domesti-
cating cats and forcing them to live in the confined quarters
of our homes. One of the reasons why veterinarians recommend that male cats be neutered at an early age is that it
allows male cats to retain their sweet personalities. Once male
cats reach puberty (around nine months of age), the surge of
testosterone racing through their veins makes them start to
feel the call of the catnip. Intact male cats are more prone to
urine mark, get into fights and roam.

PET OWNER: *A friend's dog just had a litter and I want to take*
home a puppy as soon as I can. My friend won't let me have one
until he or she is eight weeks old. Isn't it better for the pup to get
to know me sooner than that?

REPLY: Dogs and cats go through five distinct stages of development: neonatal, transitional, socialization, juvenile, and
adult. During socialization, which occurs approximately from
three to thirteen weeks of age, the personality of the pet is
shaped. Pups learn to interact with other animals, people and
the environment in an appropriate manner by watching their
litter mates and mother. Puppies that are adopted before eight
weeks of age tend to have poor people and interspecies social
skills. Most animal behaviorists will recommend that you wait

until ten to twelve weeks of age before you separate puppies from their mother and siblings (and the majority of vets prefer twelve). Another added bonus for waiting this long is the likelihood that the dog will be housebroken when you take him or her home. Housebreaking is not fun and it's ideal if it can be accomplished on someone else's carpet.

A CLIENT WITH A YOUNG FEMALE CAT CALLS. SHE WANTS TO breed the cat, but is afraid that the kitty won't be able to nurse her kittens due to her very small nipples. The woman asks, "Is it safe to breed her? Her boobs are very hard to find amongst all her long fur."

Even the most brassiere-challenged woman has experienced the breast-enhancing properties of pregnancy. Cats and dogs undergo a process called pinking up during the second or third week of gestation. During this time, the nipples change color from the typical pink to brown. In cats, an obvious enlargement of the breast tissue occurs approximately seven days before queening. Trimming the belly fur of long-haired cats will be greatly appreciated by the newborns.

PET OWNER: *I think my male cat is a homosexual. Every night, he sleeps between my husband and myself. He nestles in my husband's armpit and starts to knead with his front paws and drools. Should I scold my cat or my husband?*

REPLY: Kneading and nursing go paw in paw. When kittens are at their mother's teat, they massage the breast with their feet to increase milk flow to the glands. Later in life, when your cat is relaxed and feeling loved it will revert to this childlike behavior. So the good news is that there is no need to reprimand your husband or your cat. If you're feeling left out, start a ménage a trois by snuggling close at the other arm.

A WOMAN ENTERS THE OFFICE AND ASKS THE RECEPTIONIST IF WE sell breast pumps for cats. Her cat recently gave birth to two kittens and is beginning to show signs of going back into heat. "Isn't it true, " she inquires, "that a nursing queen will not come back in to heat? I read it on the Internet."

Envision sucking a golf ball through a garden hose and you will have an inkling of the vacuum power that a human breast pump can produce. These mechanical devices mean business. No such device exists for cats. Never try to manually milk your cat. It's just not done. There is validity to the nursing notion, albeit this woman learned about it online (be very careful, there's a lot of misinformation in cyberspace!). Typically, cats will not cycle back into season while they have suckling offspring. But if the queen has only one or two kittens, she may entertain the idea of coitus a mere seven to ten days after giving birth.

PET OWNER: *I think my cat needs Prozac. I raised him from the time that he was only three weeks of age, bottle-feeding him and everything. Initially he was a very sweet, playful kitten. Suddenly, when he reached a year of age, he became neurotic. Quick movements and even walking through the house with shoes on will result in him heading for the closet. My husband wants to give the cat away. I want to give my husband away. What can I do?*

REPLY: Good husbands are hard to find, so if this problem with the cat is your husband's only shortcoming, I'd recommend keeping both of them. Cats, like dogs, have a very definite period of socialization in their first few weeks of life. This is why it's important, whenever possible, to keep kittens with their queen and siblings until they are ten to twelve weeks of age. A normal socialization process begins twenty-one days after birth and kittens are most responsive to new persons, pets and stimuli during the critical early weeks of their lives. If you want a cat to be more confident, socially competent and sexually well adjusted, it is best to expose a kitten to a myriad of novel persons and situations while he or she remains within the feline family unit. For this woman's troubled kitty, there are medications that may be of assistance, but don't expect the answer to reside solely in a pill. Slowly, quietly and repeatedly show your cat that you are someone that he does not have to fear. Contact a veterinarian who specializes in behavioral medicine and, in the meantime, try wearing slippers around the house.

A CALLER WHO SOUNDS LIKE A VERY YOUNG GIRL IS CRYING AS SHE tells me that her German Shepherd just gave birth to nine puppies. Her mom is not home and she's afraid that when her mother returns she'll insist all the puppies be put to sleep. "Why?" I ask. She replies with a sob, "They're all blind, none of the puppies have eyes!"

Puppies and kittens are born with their eyes and ears

sealed shut. Do not try to pry them open; they will open on their own at five to fourteen days of age. Also, all puppies and kittens have blue eyes that will change to their adult color in several weeks or sometimes even later (as long as three to four months occasionally). Don't be surprised if the newborns seem to have poor vision at first. Their visual acuity will improve with age.

 **JUST THE FACTS**

A queen and bitch will continue to have estrous cycles throughout their lives. As long as general health is good and groceries in ready supply, female dogs and cats can bear young well into their senior years. A dog's bloody show may be dramatically reduced as she ages, leading some owners to believe that their dog has experienced menopause. Dogs and cats do not undergo menopause. However, as pets age, chances of complications with pregnancy and delivery increase.

Cats and dogs have a paw up when it comes to the continuation of their species due to their capacity to bear multiple litters of offspring in rather quick succession. For instance, a single cat can mother more than one hundred kittens in her lifetime. Pet caregivers may have the best of intentions when they breed their beloved furry child, but consider the number of offspring that her progeny can bring forth and it becomes very clear why pet overpopulation is out of control. It is not just the mixed breed, mutt or domestic meow that you find on death row in animal control facilities throughout the United States—purebred, pedigreed animals are destroyed in alarmingly high numbers as well.

The first several weeks of a pet's life are critical in establishing his or her personality. Kittens and puppies first enter the world blind and deaf. Contact with siblings and humans is essential during the first eight to twelve weeks. Whenever possible, these toddling fur balls should stay with the litter until they reach a minimum of eight weeks of age (although most pros prefer twelve).

Just like little humans, puppies and kittens require a series of vaccines. Other routine services that need to be addressed during their first year of life are precautionary deworming, behavioral modification (training) and neutering.

CHAPTER 5

SNIP AND TUCK

BEING A FEMALE VETERINARIAN CAN PRESENT CERTAIN obstacles. When the subject of neutering is broached, I often get the impression that male pet owners view me as the veterinary equivalent of Lorena Bobbit, the woman who cut off her husband's member. These men are easy to spot in the reception area of my hospital—they are the ones with the pained look on their faces and a distinctive stiff-legged gait. This particular style of walking is the result of pressing their thighs close together in a testicularly protective manner. No matter how many times I tell them, "I don't want your testicles, just your dog's," they clearly don't believe me. These male pet owners stare at me with a mixture of disbelief and gratitude when I inform them that neutering a pet will not lead to their own impotence. Ovaries and testicles hold mystical qualities for many pet owners, who seem to think that these few ounces of tissue impart characteristics ranging from wisdom and ferocity to serenity and steadfastness. What makes a pet a good guard dog, a loving companion or a champion working dog is not a matter of what is located between his or her legs but what exists between their ears.

The biggest misconception about neutering (this term encompasses the surgical removal of sex organs for either males or females) is that you are taking away your pet's paternal or maternal leanings by removing their reproductive abilities and that this denies him or her an essential part of life. Excuse me, but I know many humans who have never had children and are very happy with their decision. I also know several men and women who have had offspring and, in their most honest moments, wish they hadn't. Reproduction of the species isn't for everyone, and while some people might rather die than lose their reproductive abilities, pets are not troubled by such emotions. In fact, your pet won't regret never having had carnal relations or a litter of little ones. Plus, pet overpopulation is a catastrophic problem in the United States, and we should be doing everything we can to take care of the cats and dogs that currently need homes, rather than bringing even more unwanted animals into the world. Even if your pet is a blue blooded, card-carrying descendant of champion stock, there are shelters full of similar pets.

Aside from the horrible problem of pet overpopulation, there are many other reasons to neuter your pet, including tremendous health benefits. Spaying female dogs can decrease their chances of developing breast cancer, and male cats and dogs are calmed by reducing the amount of testosterone in their systems. Many of the more dangerous secondary sex characteristics of males, such as fighting and roaming, are reduced by castration.

Some owners think so highly of their dog or cat that they want to produce more just like him or her. And while your Bingo may be so charming he makes Lassie look like an ill-tempered mutt, remember it's nature and nurture that led to his unique personality. There are no guarantees that breeding will spawn similarly princely pups. And as for those folks who want to breed their pets so their children can witness firsthand the miracle of life; rent a video—it's less of a commitment, cheaper and infinitely repeatable, provided they even make it through watching the event once.

I WAS GIVING MY USUAL "PUPPY CARE 101" SPIEL TO SOME NEW clients, a young husband and wife with a new male puppy, when the husband suddenly went silent. He had been very animated, and even monopolized the conversation, until I got to the subject of neutering the dog. While he went pale, his wife appeared over-ly interested in all the details surrounding the surgery. She asked in-depth questions, such as "Where is the incision made?" and "What do you do with the testicle afterwards?" Her now-mute husband looked like he was about to faint. Then in a very pained voice he asked, "Is this what they do to a man when he gets a vasectomy?" His weird behavior suddenly made sense—he was scheduled to be snipped himself and didn't have the nerve to ask his doctor for specifics!

For some people (especially men), the word "castration" inspires a pain in the groin and a clutching of their family jew-els. Because the word is repugnant to so many, a more political-ly correct term for the procedure is "neutered" or "fixed" (the same terms can be used when referring to an ovario-hysterecto-my or spay procedure for a female). When a male animal is fixed, both testes are removed. Without testes, sperm production ceas-es and there is a major reduction of male hormones circulating in the bloodstream (testosterone is produced in small amounts by other glands in the body). A human vasectomy is an entirely dif-ferent surgical procedure where the vas deferens, the tubing that takes the sperm from the testes to the penis, is cut. This surgery is performed as a means of human male birth control, but leaves all the "maleness" afforded by testosterone intact. Because of the psychological and physiological benefits afforded by the removal of the testes, vasectomies are not routinely performed for pets.

I always stress that my clients spay their female pets and neuter their male pets as early as possible, but I was surprised when a client who owned a diminutive Pekinese puppy wanted me to spay her dog at six weeks of age. "Can't you fix her right away?" she asked, " I want her to stay as petite as possible."

Spaying a dog at an early age will not stunt its growth. What determines a pet's adult size is a function of genetics and nutrition. Many animal control agencies require that a pet be rendered incapable of reproduction before being adopted. This often necessitates that puppies and kittens as young as six weeks of age undergo neutering. After exhaustive research, this technique has been shown to be safe and does not have adverse long-term side effects. For privately-owned animals, having them spayed or castrated before they reach puberty is most common.

PET OWNER: *I read on the Internet that if I have my cat neutered too early it will stunt his growth. Is that true? I want to be a good cat owner but I don't want my cat to have a little pecker.*

REPLY: Once again, spaying or castrating your critter will not stunt its growth, including the size of this pussy's pecker. Size is determined by genetics and nutrition, not the length of time the testicles are in residence. What will be affected, however, are secondary sexual characteristics such as (for cats) penile barbs. These barbs, which excite nerve endings in the female's vagina and stimulate the ovaries to release eggs, are sometimes referred to as "feline French ticklers." If a cat is neutered before puberty, these barbs will be present but less pronounced.

A MAN CALLS INQUIRING ABOUT THE COST OF NEUTERING HIS CAT.

His response to the price quote is "Wow, that is pretty expensive. Can't you just buy a kit or something at Wal-Mart and do it yourself?"

While it might appeal to one's twisted sense of humor to contemplate just how a late night infomercial would sell a "do-it-yourself-castration kit," I'm here to tell you attempting to perform any surgical procedure at home is a really, really bad idea. Not to mention the fact that I've had cat owners who thought they owned a Sam when it was a Samantha. I tremble to think what they would try in the confines of their own abode if such a castration kit were available. Thankfully there are no such items at Wal-Mart or elsewhere, and I'm hopeful there never will be one.

Some folks may think that performing surgery on your own animal is illegal; unfortunately it is not. In most jurisdictions, animals are considered personal property, so you can do what you want with them, but that means within the realm of humane treatment. Laws dictate that animals be treated humanely. The caveat for the masses: "don't try this at home."

PET OWNER: *I've been calling around and the price to get my dog fixed seems to vary from vet to vet. Is it okay if I go with the discount clinic?*

REPLY: "Fixing" or "altering" is either spaying for the female or castration for males; both are surgical procedures that require a sterile environment and medical expertise. Prices for either procedure will vary throughout the United States, and shopping around for the cheapest fee is not always in your pet's best interest. If you find a price that is markedly below the other prices in your area, start asking questions. What type of anesthesia is being used? Does the veterinarian use newly-sterilized instruments for each pet? What types of monitoring safeguards are utilized during surgery? Is pain medication administered before, during and after surgery? Is pain medication dispensed for home use once the pet is released from the hospital?

Basically, you get what you pay for and it isn't worth the money you save to take chances with your pet's health. Also, if your pet is older or has preexisting medical concerns the fee may be higher. And while anesthesia is extremely safe nowadays, you still may want to ask your veterinarian about pre-anesthetic blood panels to screen for underlying, occult diseases in your pet that can affect the manner in which an animal reacts to anesthesia.

But don't get me wrong: there are some excellent spay and neuter clinics that provide safe and clean surgical care for dogs and cats and charge significantly less than full-service hospitals. These clinics are often associated with shelters or nonprofit groups.

OUR COMMUNITY HOUSES A LARGE AIR FORCE TRAINING BASE where many German military personnel live. A tall German Air Force officer came into the office with questions regarding the castration of his dog and the conversation went like this:

OFFICER: *I have a dog that I need to be, you know, not able to make babies.*
RECEPTIONIST: *You have a male or a female dog?*

OFFICER: *He's a male.*
RECEPTIONIST: *That would be a castration. The cost for the surgery would depend on his weight.*
The officer's face turned bright red.
OFFICER: *You mean how much the . . . you know, the balls weigh?*
RECEPTIONIST: *No sir, the entire dog!*

By the end of the interaction, my receptionist's face was as crimson as the officer's. I've always wondered what kind of diet he might have been thinking he could put the dog on to get a lower price!

Dogs and cats can be spayed or castrated as soon as they are born. However, surgery is not usually performed on newborns due to concerns about anesthesia. Early spay and neuter programs that sterilize puppies and kittens as young as six weeks old have become popular at many animal shelters. Even though the new owner of an animal adopted from a shelter may have the best intentions to have their pet altered before the pet becomes sexually active, accidental pregnancies are all too common. Extensive studies have proven that a pet's long-term health is not detrimentally impacted by this early-age procedure. Though the parts may be small, a skilled veterinarian can perform the surgery—usually in less than thirty minutes.

PET OWNER: *Will my Siamese's eyes uncross after he is neutered?*

REPLY: Well, a veterinarian does need to tug a bit on the testes as they are being removed from the scrotal sac, but not that hard. Have you ever noticed during a football game that a player grabs his belly when he "gets his bell rung?" He's not just trying to be polite—that's really where it hurts. The testes, like the ovaries, were formed in the abdominal cavity during fetal development, but migrated to the outside of the body before birth. When a man gets kicked down there, he feels it in his gut. And though getting kicked in the balls may cause a man to momentarily cross his eyes, getting them removed is not going to straighten this kitty's vision.

A MAN BRINGS IN HIS DOG THAT WAS SPAYED A YEAR EARLIER. "CAN you reverse the surgery?" he asks, "We want to breed her."

Once the plumbing is gone, it cannot be reinstalled. A spay for a dog or a cat is an ovario-hysterectomy, a surgical removal of the entire uterus and both ovaries. There is no reversal or way to reinstall these reproductive organs. Aside from preventing pregnancies, a spay rids females of the hormones (produced by the ovaries) that contribute to breast cancer and ovarian cancer. Also, without these hormones, bitches and queens are calmer and less likely to roam when they are in the throes of their sexual urges experienced during estrus.

PET OWNER: *I don't think you neutered him right. He has these two balls on his penis that get bigger when I rub on them. Do you think they have grown back?*

Dog testicles are not lizard tails—they don't grow back. Castration is a very straightforward procedure: the surgeon removes the two testicles. I have heard of people who wanted to keep them as a memento. (Maybe they had them bronzed; I really didn't want to know.) This pet owner spotted the dog's two bulbourethral glands located on the sides of the penile shaft. These paired glands produce fluid that comprises part of the ejaculate, which in an unaltered dog includes fluid secreted by the prostate, bulbourethral glands, seminal vesicles, and semen with its nutrient plasma. Even after the testes are removed, the bulbourethral gland can swell in size if a dog becomes excited.

PET OWNER: *Can you neuter him again? He is still humping!*

REPLY: Testicles have nothing to do with pelvic gyrations. Mounting is an act of machismo and dominance, and both male and female dogs do it to demonstrate superiority. However, having a canine neutered before puberty will often curtail this indecorous act.

PET OWNER: *If I neuter my cat, will he still catch rats?*

REPLY: That depends on why he is catching them! Testes and ovaries have nothing to do with the hunting instinct in cats. In fact, even hunger has little effect; many cats will stalk and collar prey just for the fun of it.

PET OWNER: *If I have my cat neutered, can he still fight?*

REPLY: Yes, provided he fights with his teeth and claws and not his balls. Cat combat is not solely a function of testosterone, but the hormone does play a major role in cats' desire to get into spats. Intact males are more likely to try to defend their territory and their chosen mates. Neutered males and spayed females can still tousle, but this is often a matter of close quarters and other psychological stressors.

PET OWNER: *If I have my cat neutered, will he still go out at night?*

REPLY: Yes, but he will only be able to serve as a consultant. Neutering a cat will dramatically reduce its desire to roam, but the feline's basic nature remains. And we all know what a cat's credo is: Sleep all day, play all night. Keeping cats indoors has been shown to increase both their longevity and waistlines.

Remember, housebound cats should be fed commensurate with their level of activity and age to help guard against the silent killer, obesity. It is estimated that approximately fifty percent of adult pets in the United States are obese. Pets that are overweight put unneeded stress on their heart, joints, and internal organs. They are more prone to develop diabetes mellitus, along with weakening their immune systems. A recent long-term study has shown that dogs that stayed on the lean side their entire lives lived fifteen percent longer than their litter mates who ate to their tummy's content. America's pets (and people) are experiencing the adverse side effects of super-sized meals and treats and a lack of exercise. If you are not sure if your pet is fluffy or fat, make an appointment with your veterinarian.

AS I ENTERED THE EXAM ROOM, I KNEW IT WAS NOT GOING TO GO smoothly. The husband and wife were arguing vehemently about getting their five-month-old Irish setter neutered. The sticking point was the fact that the man once had a dog die while under anesthesia years ago. He said he would not have a dog neutered until veterinary medicine came up with a drive-thru castration. I smiled and asked him, "So, do you want fries with that order?"

While you won't get any fries with it, chemical castration is now a reality and it's the closest thing to a "drive-thru castration" you can get. The process works by an injection of zinc gluconate into each testicle. The needle is very fine and the amount of material injected is small, so the injection is not painful, especially because, believe it or not, the testes do not contain pain receptors. (However, testes do possess nerve endings that are sensitive to pressure. Whack them hard enough and I don't think a male can tell the difference between pressure and pain!) Following the injection, the testes may swell a bit and then slowly atrophy. Soon they cease producing sperm altogether.

Unlike surgical castration, the testosterone created in the testes is not eradicated so behaviors like roaming, mounting, and urine marking will persist after the chemical process. It is recommended that chemically neutered males be kept away from breedable females for at least sixty days post injection to ensure that the pet is sperm free, and there are age limitations and testicular size requirements for the process. So, if you just can't bear the thought of surgery or the sight of your dog's thighs rubbing together when his manhood is removed (he's left with a small cushion post-chemical castration), this FDA approved procedure is for you.

PET OWNER: *My three-year-old Border Collie mix was spayed before her first period. Whenever I rub her belly, I feel these long lumps on either side of where the incision was made. Is this breast cancer?*

REPLY: If your darling has a lack of body fat, and you are feeling a single row of bumps under the skin, you may simply be feeling the sutures from the surgery on the underlying linea alba. The linea alba is a white line that runs down the belly wall, under the skin, where the muscles from either side of the abdomen meet. This line does not contain blood vessels, so it is a perfect spot for a veterinary surgeon to enter the abdominal cavity.

Spaying a dog before its first estrous cycle can dramatically reduce the chances of her developing breast cancer later in life, but it is not a guarantee. Since this Border Collie is only three years of age, it is unlikely that the lumps that you are feeling are cancerous. Most likely what you are feeling are fat deposits under the skin. As a general rule, if you feel lumps on your pet that are on opposite sides of the body and in the same general location and feel similar in character, they are probably not cancerous. When in doubt, though, see your veterinarian. A simple test, known as a fine-needle aspirate, can be performed to help determine the real identity of the mass. It can often be done without anesthesia while you wait.

A WOMAN ON THE PHONE WHO OWNS A TWO-YEAR-OLD YORKSHIRE Terrier that was spayed says that her dog is now in heat. "Do you think her girl parts grew back?" she wants to know.

If this dog were truly showing signs of being "in heat" (in the state of estrus) it wouldn't be because the "girl parts" grew back. More likely, a bit of hormone-producing tissue was accidentally trapped within the suture material that the veterinarian placed at the base of the ovary prior to cutting it free from the body, during the ovario-hysterectomy. Though the total amount of ovarian tissue may be small, it could be enough to produce sufficient quantities of female hormones that would trigger an estrous cycle. A rare female cat or dog may also have aberrant ovarian tissue that is located at other sites in the abdomen aside from the ovaries—German Shepherds, for example, are commonly found to possess these extra hormone-producing sites.

Though a pet may have signs of being in heat and may even allow breeding, a spayed pet cannot become pregnant because she has no uterus. Perhaps it is helpful to think of this case as similar to a woman who has had a hysterectomy, but her ovaries are left in place. She can still experience PMS (pre-menstrual syndrome) even though there will never be a menstrual cycle.

Also, in the case of this terrier, there are other conditions that can mimic an estrous cycle. Bleeding from the vaginal area might also be a sign of trouble in the urinary tract or vagina. A thorough veterinary exam may be needed.

A CAT IS PRESENTED TO ME THAT NEEDED TREATMENT FOR A laceration on his scrotum. When I asked the owner how this injury happened, he told me he tried to neuter his cat the way his granddaddy taught him. He had stuck the cat's head in a boot and then "had at it" with a penknife. He was genuinely puzzled as to what was wrong with his surgical technique. I was tempted to have him drop his pants, stick his head in a trashcan and show him.

Thank goodness some of the less savory farm-style methods of animal husbandry are dying out. It may be tempting to save a few bucks and try to neuter your cat at home, but don't. Though your pet may not be able to verbalize that it feels pain (although I'm sure cutting off your cat's balls would cause more than just a howl of protest) cats and dogs are basically wired the same way we are. If you think a procedure would cause you discomfort, it will likely cause pain for your pet. And don't forget the potential of infection that could lead to illness or even the death of your pet. Don't do it!!!

THE POOR LITTLE DOG HAD BEEN MINDING HER OWN BUSINESS, walking on her leash with her owner. But as they crossed the street, a car screeched around the corner and hit the dog. The pooch sustained a badly fractured pelvis and a crushed neck of the femur. I explained to the owner that cage rest would allow the pelvis to heal but since the hip is a ball-and-socket joint, the only way that the pet ever stood a chance to walk without pain was to surgically remove the head of the femur. The surgical approach to the area of the hip joint is a small incision over the upper aspect of the thigh. As I was about to leave to begin the surgery, I asked her if she had any questions, and the woman replied, "I've been meaning to spay her but haven't gotten around to it. Could you spay her through the same incision line? I don't want her to lose too much fur."

This pup would be best served by allowing the pet to recover from the stress of the trauma and spay her at a later date. Plus, the typical incision for a spay is made on the centerline of the belly (ventral midline or linea alba) with the incision going toward the head and tail rather than side-to-side. A flank approach (an incision made on the side of the body) is possible, but is more difficult. The skin incision to access the fractured femur in this case is very superficial and would be located over the hip joint—you just couldn't reach the organs we need for a spay from way up there.

Prior to a spay, pet owners frequently ask about the size of the incision. My usual response is, "The incision will be as big as it needs to be so I can safely see what I am doing." Dogs and cats are not as vain as you and I can be—they don't wear G-string swimwear and they are covered with fur, so scar size is simply not an issue.

PET OWNER: *Can you spay them while they're in heat? I've heard that it messes up their hormones and changes their personalities.*

REPLY: Yes, you can spay them while they are in heat, but it is more difficult. One of the main reasons to spay a pet is to remove the negative influences of the reproductive hormones. By eradicating these chemical messengers of lust and desire, a pet owner can decrease the chances that a pet in the throes of hormonal frenzy will run the streets looking for love but find the underside of a car's tire by mistake. Your veterinarian may charge more for a spay if your pet is in heat because the vessels to the ovaries and uterus are engorged with blood, making the procedure time-intensive.

A FEMALE DOG OWNER IS IN A CONUNDRUM: SHE WANTS TO HAVE HER dog castrated but her husband is adamantly against it. She thinks she can conceal the surgery from her spouse by testicular implants. I tell her the price of such cosmetics and she reacts with chagrin, "Fake balls cost that much! Can't I bring in a couple of golf balls and you use them in instead?"

That's right, silicone implants are not just for people anymore—even veterinary medicine has gotten into the act. The ultimate vanity accessory for the altered male pooch is fake balls. These silicone prostheses, which have the texture of gummy bears, can be implanted at the time of a dog's surgical castration. Do dogs really need fake balls? Of course not, but many owners are mesmerized by the swaying of their pooch's pouches, be it real or not.

PET OWNER: *Do you remove the penis when you neuter him?*

REPLY: No, a veterinarian does not remove the penis when a pet is neutered, only the testicles are surgically removed—this person must never have investigated the underside of a fixed dog. While a dog's penis can be removed for medical reasons such as tumors or blockages of the urethra, such a procedure is highly unusual.

OFTEN PEOPLE WILL WANT TO HAVE THEIR DOG NEUTERED AT AN early age because they are attempting to curtail the act of leg lifting and urine marking. Sometimes it helps but not always. Both behaviors are considered secondary male sex characteristics but even females will occasionally perform these same acts. Why? No one really knows for sure. A secondary sexual characteristic of an intact male cat is a very pungent urine odor, so intact toms love to mark their territories with it. People often mistakenly think that cats are spraying some special liquid when they mark, but nope, it's just regular cat piss. And toms also benefit from a unique anatomical positioning of the penis, so that when they let loose, the stinky stuff is projected straight out behind them in a horizontal stream.

I WAS PERFORMING A "WELLNESS EXAMINATION" ON A MORBIDLY obese Lab. The owner, who was on the portly side himself, swore the Lab was full-figured because she had been spayed. "I'll never get one of my dogs spayed again. When I was growing up on the farm, we never had them fixed and they never got fat. Doesn't spaying them always make them fat?"

What makes a pet fat is, as a rule, the pet owner. A dog or cat is generally neutered around the time of puberty. Besides heralding sexual maturity, puberty also marks the end of their rapid growth phase. It is true that once the gonads (ovaries or testes) are removed, the metabolism does slow. The degree to which it dawdles is minimal. Pet owners need to remember that their pets are no longer "growing babies" and feed their charges in accordance to their lifestyle. Recent studies have shown that slimmer pets will outlive their corpulent relatives by as much as fifteen percent.

I KNEW THIS WAS GOING TO BE AN EXAM TO REMEMBER AS I TRIED not to laugh at the comical sight that greeted me as I walked in to the examination room: a hundred-pound female Akita wearing men's BVD undies with her tail sticking out of the front opening. All the while she was gaily whooshing her tail to and fro unaware of the impact of her appearance. Her distressed owner, clearly at the end of his rope, said defensively, "But Doc, what else could I do? She has been wetting the bed every night!"

A complete exam and analysis of the dog's medical history revealed that this spayed bitch was exhibiting signs of hormonal urinary incontinence—when the pet was sleeping or deeply relaxed she would dribble urine. This situation might have gone unnoticed if the dog had been a Teacup Poodle or slept on the floor, but the size of this dog, and the fact that she slept on the bed with the owner at night made the problem obvious; the dog was flooding her owner out of dreamland.

Urinary incontinence occasionally affects middle-aged to older female dogs that have been spayed, no matter at what age they were spayed. This condition can also affect older male dogs, but for different reasons. Like us, our pets become victims of gravity as they age and things start to sag—bladders, boobs, skin, etc. Also, the lack of female hormones in the mature, spayed dog can lead to weakening of the sphincters (valves) that control urine flow. These two factors combined can result in the leakage of urine while the dog is deeply relaxed or sleeping. The good news is there are medications that can tighten the valves, so Fido can still sleep beside you at night.

If you notice urine spots on your pet's bedding, you need to take him or her to the vet. There are a number of other possible causes and the veterinarian may need to perform blood and urine tests to determine the source of the problem and the best way to treat it.

JUST THE FACTS

Neutering is a generic term that includes spaying (ovario-hysterectomy) and castration (orchidectomy). Neutering can garner tremendous health benefits for both male and female cats and dogs. Spaying a female dog before her first heat cycle can decrease the incidence of breast cancer by ninety-eight percent; male dogs are often calmed by not having the circulating testosterone in their systems. Male cats are less likely to roam once they have been neutered, which helps keep them out of harm's way. Also, male cats and dogs both tend to get into fewer fights and will do less urine marking after they've "had their pockets picked." The one exception to the early neuter-and-spay rule is the female dog that shows an aggressive tendency. Some animal behaviorists speculate that these females may have been exposed to an abnormally high level of androgens when they were in the uterus. I recommend that such dogs be allowed to experience one or two estrous cycles before neutering. Neutering does slow down a pet's metabolism, but the degree to which it is stifled is minimal. What makes a pet overweight once he or she has been rendered reproductively incapable is excessive feeding—that's right, you or I constantly overfilling the food dish. Once we humans get over our own hang-ups about reproduction, we will realize that when it comes to the furry members of our families, there are many more benefits than liabilities to a little snip and tuck.

CHAPTER 6

WAGGING ON THE WILD SIDE

PETS ARE HEDONISTS AT HEART; IF IT FEELS GOOD, THEY WILL do it. And if it feels good and gets a positive response, they'll want to do it again, repeating the behavior that brought them pleasure. Sheer sensory enjoyment is high on the dog or cat to-do list, which can sometimes make for some unacceptable behaviors. Cats are notorious for enjoying leisurely skeletal elongations, stretching. (I enjoy my Hatha yoga sessions so much that I think in a prior life I may have been a feline.) Combine that stretch with the sharpening of their nails on your expensive handwoven, imported wall coverings and you have true kitty nirvana. Why do cats persist in destroying your possessions despite being threatened with domicile expulsion? Because it feels too good to cease and desist, of course. Ditto for dogs who constantly lick themselves (although often they are just taking care of hygiene issues, and aren't you glad for that? . . . better them than you!). And when it comes to canine reproductive ardor, the words decorum and dog should not be used in the same sentence. Dogs and cats will "do it" right in front of you, the neighbors, children, and anyone else who may be in the vicinity. They don't care; it feels good and it's exactly what their hormones are telling them to do.

After sensory pleasure, pleasing their owner/companion is probably next on the dog and cat to-do list. Pets strive to satisfy you, with the hopes of love, affection and, of course, rewards. If your pet is exhibiting behaviors that are undesirable, ask yourself if you may be unintentionally reconfirming to the pet that this behavior will garner gratification. Have you ever had a dog that insisted on destroying only your most expensive shoes? Sure, tearing apart stuff (too bad your mutt thinks a pair of Manolos qualify as "stuff") is an entertaining pastime for a bored Bichon, but you may have unwittingly aided and abetted this footwear fetish. When he was a teething pup, you may have inadvertently bestowed one of your old shoes or socks as a pacifier. This youngster came to associate chewing on clothing laced with your scent as a comforting, enjoyable act. For some pets, even a negative response is better than getting no attention at all. Need assistance in breaking your pet from humping your leg or mounting another pet? Ask your veterinarian for some pointers or request a referral to a board-certified veterinary behaviorist. And if you haven't gotten this book's mantra yet: for goodness sake, get your dog or cat neutered! It is a lot easier to get a pet's attention when they are not preoccupied with carnal pursuits.

Like bartenders or hairdressers, veterinarians are privy to personal information from our clients that we would often prefer not to know. Pet owners seem to feel relaxed and at ease around vets—it must be our animal magnetism. Relaxed is good; however, letting it all hang out can lead to embarrassing situations. Before I learned the hard way to carefully phrase all my questions, I had a client who brought in a terrible-looking cat whose fur seemed as if it had been attacked by a ravenous, fur-eating moth. Upon inspection, there were bald spots and crusty skin all over the cat's body. My list of possible causes included ringworm, a fungal skin disease that can be spread from pets to people. On people, ringworm results in a rather characteristic circular skin eruption that is very itchy. To help me confirm my suspicion that we were dealing with ringworm, I asked the owner if he was suffering from any type of skin problem. Immediately, he dropped his trousers and pointed to a rash, high on his inner thigh. As if that gesture wasn't enough, the owner was the type of guy who liked to dress "commando style'" (i.e., no underwear). I did my best to remain professional and recommended that he see his physician. Then, as quickly as possible, I whisked the kitty away to another room to "run some tests." Later, I asked my technician to return the cat to the client; I just couldn't face him with a straight face.

Lesson learned: all medical and veterinary students should receive instruction on phrasing questions to clients to insure there is no ambiguity in what we ask. Otherwise, the range of interpretations can lead to many misunderstandings—some hilarious, some just downright uncomfortable. But I don't think there are any classroom tips that would have helped a friend of mine while she was performing her internship for medical school in Missouri. As she was taking the medical history from a young female patient, she got to "Are you sexually active?" on the list. The patient turned to her and replied, "No, I just lie there."

PET OWNER: *My three-year-old Siamese cat has a fetish for wool. I first noticed wet spots on my wool sweaters, then socks, and eventually wool blankets. Even if I have them put away in my closet or drawers, she finds a way in to get to these places and starts sucking on them. Do I need to take her to a kitty psychologist? What's wrong with her?*

REPLY: Wool sucking may be associated with dietary deficiencies, behavioral problems such as obsessive-compulsive disorder and early weaning. Cats are reported to nurse on fabric and other inanimate objects, such as plastic, metal, or even an owner's underarms. In some Oriental breeds, such as the Siamese, suckling appears to be a hereditary condition. The act of suckling itself is not problematic, but it can lead to the ingestion of nondigestible materials and that is dangerous. Pets can basically eat two major types of non-food items: radiodense, which is visible on an X-ray, and radiolucent, which is not. If your pet has to eat something it is not supposed to, veterinarians would prefer it be radiodense so the matter can be identified on an x-ray and monitored as it transits. Wool, underwear, socks and the like, are all radiolucent, so their presence can sometimes only be established by the oral administration of liquid that will outline the foreign body, or possibly by surgical exploration.

But why do some cats like to suckle wool? Many animal behaviorists believe that the texture and scent of wet wool is reminiscent of wet feline fur. Treatment can range from drug therapy using Valium, Elavil or Doxepin, to the simple act of picking up your clothes and denying access to your woolies.

PET OWNER: *Can you tell if my husband is having sex with my dog?*

REPLY: Oh my goodness! This is the type of question that every health care professional dreads. Sometimes the question is asked for shock value alone; on other occasions the pet owner is unflinchingly serious but sadly delusional. I remember speaking with an obviously confused older client on the phone who related in explicit detail the sexual encounters her husband was having with her Miniature Schnauzer. I listened sympathetically and then asked to speak with her husband. I told him about his wife's stories, which mortified him, and he explained that she was under psychiatric care and had lost her grip on reality.

Bestiality does exist. It crosses all sociological and economic boundaries. I do not claim to be a psychiatrist or psychologist, but I will state that studies have been conducted that show that people who abuse pets are more likely to abuse people. Some states now require that if any animal health care professional suspects that an animal is being abused, they must report that person to the proper authorities. If you believe that a pet is being mistreated, seek professional assistance immediately.

PET OWNER: *I can't get my dog to stop masturbating! Can I rent a shock collar to train him not to lick himself down there?*

REPLY: Why does a dog or cat lick himself or herself "down there?" Simple, because they can! This dog may not be performing acts of self-gratification, but rather a bit of personal hygiene. If a pet has only shown mild interest in this portion of his anatomy in the past, and is now seemingly obsessed with those parts, it may be signaling a urogenital disorder. Since the bladder and male reproductive plumbing all exist through the penis, a bladder or prostrate problem can cause a penile discharge or discomfort that leads the dog to groom repeatedly. Also, some pet owners may make such a fuss over their pets humping stuffed toys, flashing a hard-on, or attending to cleanliness chores that it actually causes the dog to do it more—just to rile up the folks.

PET OWNER: *I've heard that female Beagles are more prone to lesbianism. How can I insure that my female will be attracted to males?*

REPLY: While homosexuality does exist in the animal kingdom, it is not found in cats or dogs. If an animal were truly homosexual, it would only show interest and mount those of its own sex. Remember, mounting for dogs and cats is not always a sex act; more often, it's an act to establish dominance.

THE EXAMINATION WAS UNEVENTFUL: A DOG WAS PRESENTED FOR scooting. I explained to the owner that the dog was dragging his bottom on the ground trying to relieve the pain he felt from his anal sacs being extremely full. I told her to think of the dog's condition as similar to a person with a bad case of hemorrhoids. Much to the dog's relief, I emptied the glands and both dog and owner left happy. However, the next morning as I unlocked the doors to the clinic, the phone was ringing off the hook. The caller was the spectacularly irate husband of the woman whose dog I had seen the day before for the impacted anal sacs. His wife had informed him that my diagnosis for the scooting was "full anal sex." Though I thought I had given her a detailed medical explanation of the pet's condition and had enunciated clearly, she clearly heard something quite different from "full anal sacs." Now I always refer to anal sacs as anal glands.

Western society has developed the custom of shaking hands as a greeting and the issuance of property deeds to lay claim to a piece of land. Cats and dogs greet and lay claim to territory by utilizing scent. Dogs and cats possess scent glands in various parts of their bodies: the face, the bottoms of their paws and in glands located adjacent to their rectums. The latter are the most potent (think of skunks and their penchant for explosively releasing their musk as a defensive move). The anal glands produce a fetid liquid that is stored in the glands, one on either side of the rectum. The aroma of this glandular material is unique to each pet. Humans are unable to distinguish one stinky bum from another, but dogs have a keen nose for the stuff. Dogs use this substance for marking and recognition more than cats do.

Every time a cat or dog defecates, the muscles around the rectum squeeze on these glands, coating the scat with some of this malodorous material. If the glands are not able to discharge this material appropriately, the buildup can become very uncomfortable, leading to excessive licking or scooting.

A CLIENT, REFERRING TO HER FEMALE DOG'S NON-BLOODY vaginal discharge, asks, "Is it caused by ear mites?"

Ear mites will not cause a vaginal discharge. People have accused other homo sapiens of having their heads up their rears, but this is not an admonishment typically made to a dog or cat. Yes, ear mites, also known as Otodectes cynotis, can migrate out of the ear, but generally they prefer the warm, dark, moist environment of the ear canal. But ear mites can set up residence at the base of a pet's tail because of the way our critters like to sleep in a ball with the tail wrapped around the face. This can lead to an itchy rump, as well as itchy ears. Ear mites are most commonly found in puppies and kittens but will occasionally be found in adult pets, typically when a young, new pet has recently been added to the household.

However, ear mites—even those who move south for the winter—have nothing to do with vaginal discharge. Oozing fluids of any kind from this area (other than the bloody show associated with estrus) can be the sign of a serious medical condition and merit a trip to the veterinarian. Possible conditions in this case include a bladder infection, kidney disease, uterine disorders, vaginal infections or conformational abnormalities that can lead to skin infections near the vulva. I have even treated a dog that was presented for having a gooey vaginal discharge that was caused by her misfortune of sitting on a foxtail, a weed with a very sharp, pointy tip. It migrated up her vagina where it started to fester. Ouch!

IT IS NOT UNCOMMON FOR CLIENTS TO WALK INTO THE CLINIC without an appointment, but this young woman was someone we had never seen before. She didn't even bring a pet with her, instead saying she needed only to ask the doctor a question. When queried by the receptionist about her inquiry, she refused to answer any questions. In a sheepish tone, she requested that the veterinarian be a "lady doctor." As I walked into the examination room, the woman was fumbling with her purse and declined to look me in the eye. Before I could say anything, she blurted out "Can a person catch crabs from a cat? My boyfriend told me he got it from his kitty."

Sure, a person can catch crabs from a pussy, just not a felis cattus (domestic tabby). Genital lice (pthirus pubis) are solely a homo sapiens problem. This external parasite resides in the hair of the pubic region but can also take up housekeeping in a person's eyebrows (I don't want to know how they got there!). To give the boyfriend the benefit of the doubt, there are a few other ways to contract genital lice, including dirty bed linens and soiled clothing. But he definitely did not contract them from a kitty cat.

AFTER I DIAGNOSED A MALE CLIENT'S DOG WITH A YEAST INFECTION in the ears, the man, astonished at the news, asked, "Wow, my girlfriend just found out from her OB/GYN that she has a yeast infection. Are the two problems related?"

This query brings to mind another story. A female client, when told that her dog, which was a chronic paw licker, had a yeast infection between its toes, inquired if she may have given the dog the malady. She confessed that she often enjoyed watching television in the nude and her dog always sat on the couch next to her. She was recovering from a vaginal yeast infection and felt badly that maybe she was responsible.

Yeast is a type of fungus, a single-celled organism that reproduces by budding. It is a ubiquitous entity that is responsible for everything from the fermentation of sugar into alcohol to the leavening of dough into bread. It is also responsible for an itchy, stinky skin infection in dogs and cats called Malassezia-induced dermatitis. The Malassezia organism does not affect normal skin, but once a pet's excessive scratching or licking damages the skin, fungal infections are common. Excessive paw licking is frequently seen as a response to allergies.

A different type of organism, Candida, causes human vaginal yeast infections. This owner's inclination to lounge in the buff did not cause her canine companion's dermal dilemma, but it might not be a bad idea for her to invest in some slipcovers.

I WAS WORKING AT THE LOCAL EMERGENCY CLINIC ON A QUIET night. Around midnight, a man with a small Poodle came in. He had the dog wrapped in a blanket, as you would a human baby. It was obvious from the start that the one in distress was the owner, not the dog. He demanded that he see a male doctor. He was out of luck, because I was the only vet on duty. He begrudgingly acquiesced and slowly unwrapped the dog from the blanket. I immediately saw the problem: the dog had an erection that would not stop. The penis was engorged, deep pink in color, and had a very dry appearance. I noticed a cowlick of long fur at the end of the dog's sheath, which was wrapped around the head of the penis, causing the prepuce to act as a constricting band. This poor pup's penis could not be retracted into the safe, warm harbor of his sheath.

This dog's condition, known as paraphimosis, was alleviated by a cold shower, some K-Y Jelly and a haircut. Though human males may resort to the use of pliable rings placed on their turgid members to prolong their erections, dogs do not need such sexual aids. Transient paraphimosis is common in dogs and is associated with canine coitus. Though dogs always have an erection because of the os penis, the penis is normally enveloped within its sheath. During times of excitement, especially as in mating, additional erectile tissue associated with the penis becomes engorged with blood, causing the penis to extend beyond the end of the prepuce. If paraphimosis continues for too long a time, the erectile tissue of the penis can become irreversibly damaged, preventing the canine penis from moving normally in and out of the sheath. If the penis becomes too badly desiccated from extended exposure, amputation may be necessary.

THE CLIENT ON THE PHONE WANTED THE NAME OF A PET PSYCHIC. She had adopted a cat from a local shelter less than a month ago. During the past month the cat had been very playful but never vicious, until last evening. The cat's owner had just gotten out of the shower and was seated on her dressing room bench drying herself when the cat jumped up between her legs and bit her. She hoped that the mentalist could provide insight into why her cat behaved in such a horrid manner.

While I do believe that some people can read a pet's body language better than others and are more intuitive in understanding a pet's psyche, this woman did not need a psychic to tell her what was going on—my degree in veterinary medicine would suffice. After, I found out the cat was an intact male I knew the reason for his aggressive act. "Are you menstruating?" I asked. Indeed, she was. Intact male cats can be attracted by the scent of menstrual discharge—her cat was simply experiencing a bit of biological friskiness. The owner made an appointment to get the cat neutered the following day.

THE INFORMATION ON THE MEDICAL HISTORY FORM SIMPLY STATED that the one-year-old Akita before me had a bladder infection. As is my habit, I start asking some background questions before examining the exuberant pet (exuberant indeed, his manhood was quite obvious). None of the owner's answers to my questions suggested that the dog was suffering from a bladder problem— he wasn't drinking any more water than usual, straining to urinate, or relieving himself more frequently. Nor were there urinary accidents in the house. I finally asked the owner what made him think there was a problem at all. He replied, "He's got this gooey discharge from the penis. Isn't that pus?"

After a thorough physical, my diagnosis was a build-up of smegma. No medication was needed; however, this pup might benefit from a doggie bidet. Smegma is a malodorous, yellow-white discharge that can build up around a male's foreskin and penis. A similar material can be found around the female's vulva, but to a lesser degree. The substance is a natural lubricant that, for the male, allows the penis to slide in and out of the prepuce (the sheath that covers the penis) easily and aids in intromission. Though it may seem immodest to some pet owners when a dog or cat cleans his genital area, he is actually keeping this discharge under control. If a young, intact male dog becomes sexually excited the amount of smegma can become copious. How can a pet parent keep this material from fouling the couch and bed-spread? Baby wipes are one alternative, although I recommend a more permanent solution: neutering.

A PET OWNER'S REACTION TO BAD NEWS CAN VARY FROM TEARS to fury, but fainting was a new one for me. I had just told this owner of a female St. Bernard that her bitch had a sexually trans-mitted disease. Before I could finish my explanation, the woman slid off of the bench in the exam room and onto the floor. The dog was equally concerned because she started enthusiastically lick-ing her owner's face. The woman was revived, but still pale when she asked, "Did my dog get this disease from my husband or another dog?"

This woman does not have to fear that the human animal

bond between her husband and dog has strayed into the realm of inappropriate conduct. A dog contracts a STD (sexually transmitted disease) by having intercourse with another dog that is infected with the organism Brucella canis. This organism can also be found in the nasal passages, mouth, and eyes of infected canines. Studies have shown that when infected and non-infected dogs of the same sex were kenneled together for extended periods of time, the non-infected dogs did not contract the disease.

The symptoms that a dog will exhibit with this disease can be quite varied. A dog may be listless, show exercise intolerance, develop meningitis or merely have a poor haircoat. The most common and most serious problem for a bitch that is being used for breeding is spontaneous abortion or resorption of the pups toward the end of her pregnancy. If the bitch has a full-term pregnancy, the puppies she delivers may be alive or dead. A female dog that fails to conceive may be afflicted with Brucellosis and reabsorb the feti before showing any signs of pregnancy.

There are several different types of diagnostic tests that can be performed if this disease is present. Antibiotics are not always effective against the organism and at the present, there are no vaccines to prevent it. Most veterinarians will recommend that an infected dog not be used for breeding. And though the incidence is extremely rare, the organism can be spread to humans. Owners of infected dogs need to practice good hygiene to avoid transmission.

SHE WAS AMAZING TO BEHOLD—MY GRANDMOTHER WOULD HAVE described this female client as "well heeled." She was perfectly groomed; her fingernails were painted a bright pink, not a chip to be seen, and her makeup was subtle but spectacular. The woman's dress suggested a two-martini lunch with friends at some chic restaurant. I was impressed. The client's kitty however, was another story. There was a definite malodor to the cat and he vigorously licked his heiny on the exam room table. Closer examination revealed that one of his anal sacs had ruptured and was oozing infected goo. When I explained the situation, the woman loudly exclaimed in a gravelly voice, "You mean he's a backdoor kind of boy?" Poof, went the illusion of her class.

Homosexuality occurs in the animal kingdom, but not in cats. One male may mount another, but as I have stated before, it is typically to demonstrate dominance rather than sexual interest. A cat's anal sacs are located at the three and nine o'clock position of the rectum (the tail is at twelve). Every time a dog or cat defecates, the muscles around the rectum squeeze down on the gland and push some of the glandular material onto the stool. Anal glands can become infected, making the normally liquid glandular material thick like toothpaste, and preventing it from being pushed out of the glands. The ducts may also become clogged or occluded by a buildup of fecal material in the opening or by tumors pressing on the duct. When this occurs, the sac may enlarge to the point of rupturing, which is as painful as it sounds. Treatment depends on the severity of the abscess, but often requires wound care and antibiotics.

JUST THE FACTS

With domestication, humans have modified the sexual behaviors and reproductive cycles of cats and dogs. The ancestors of our pets, the wolf and the lion, are subject to the vagaries of environmental and societal conditions. If there is not enough food to support the offspring, the animals with less standing in the pack or pride either do not come into season, have false pregnancies, or don't breed at all. The once-yearly estrous cycle of wolves and lions has evolved into the twice-annual pattern we now see in our house pets. This evolution occurred quickly due to an abundance of food and lack of regulating factors. With this newfound sexual activity has come the dilemma of pet overpopulation.

The close relationship people have with their pets is leading to clashes in how we expect our pets to deport themselves and their hormone-induced reality. Recent studies have shown that there are hundreds of thousands of pets that are euthanized on a yearly basis in the United States because of misunderstood behavioral issues. This is a travesty and a tragedy. Early spaying and castration can usually alleviate many of these concerns. While neutering does not guarantee that "objectionable conduct" (to us, that is—to our pets it's simply natural) will not ensue, but veterinarians do know that removing the hormones that cause these behaviors often helps.

Our furry friends supply us with unquestioning acceptance and unconditional love. In return, we must provide them with a safe haven, proper nutrition, access to appropriate medical care, and, of course, we must love them right back.

CHAPTER 7

ANATOMY 101

THE CAT

PROFESSOR PATCHES

SK ANY KINDERGARTENER WHERE HIS OR HER NOSE, MOUTH, or heart is located and they will get it right nine out of ten times. But ask a pet owner where a dog's or cat's bladder or liver resides in their furry friend's body and most haven't a clue. Our basic knowledge of anatomy is shot when it comes to fur-covered creatures with a four-legged stance.

This may come as a surprise to some, but cats and dogs are mammals—as are humans. Webster defines a mammal as a "warm-blooded vertebrate that nourishes its young with milk secreted by mammary glands and having skin, more or less, covered with hair." In general, pets are constructed in a similar manner to their human caregivers. The exact arrangement of the components is modified, but for the most part you're dealing with the same parts in different places. Things look a little different, too. Now I will freely admit that I am "automobile challenged." My poor mechanic dreads when I drive up with the complaint that there is a weird "cachunka-chunka" sound coming from somewhere near that black "dooflachee" near that shiny "whoza-witz" with all the wires coming out of it. It is probably a matter of cosmic payback whenever I am told by a pet owner that a certain, lump, bump or other malady is plaguing their furry charge on a particular side of its body (then I search in vain, totally unable to find it). It is at times like this that I start to doubt my medical acumen. Inevitably the owners pipes up, "No doc, not that side—the other side." I can't tell you how many times I have had to tell an owner, "Pretend you are the pet. Now what side of the body is having the problem?"

Even when someone might know the correct medical terminology for an anatomical entity or bodily function, people tend

116

to use euphemisms because the real word seems politically incorrect. For many people it sounds "nicer" to say "pee pee" or "poop" rather than "urinate" or "defecate." But knowing the correct names of pet body parts, instead of referring to "you whos" and "thingies" can alleviate major misunderstandings. I once had a sweet older lady drop off her dog for an examination who told the receptionist that the pet was suffering from a problem "down there." Well, I looked "down there" and found a mass on one of the dog's testicles. With the age of the dog and the changes that were present, I was concerned that it might be cancer. I prepared an estimate of charges for a thorough diagnostic workup that included neutering the pet and having the affected testicle analyzed. When I called the woman on the phone and gave her the estimate, she became irate. Turns out she was concerned with a small wart on the dog's bum and had no interest in addressing any other problems. We all have our own priorities, and hers was a dog with a pretty bum. Go figure!

PET OWNER: *How can my cat be a boy? He has nipples!*

REPLY: I get this question from both men and women and it always makes me laugh. I usually respond by asking the client if they have ever been to the beach or swimming pool. At varying rates, you can see the dawning of enlightenment when they suddenly realize that men have nipples too. Well, the same goes for male dogs and cats, although granted, in all cases male mammary tissue is solely ornamental.

AN UNSPAYED FEMALE LABRADOR RETRIEVER WAS PRESENTED for a bladder infection. The owner had noted a fetid discharge from the dog's vulva. The dog had been in heat approximately six weeks earlier. After a blood and urine analysis, plus abdominal x-rays, I determined that she was suffering from an infection-filled uterus (pyometra) and not a bladder disease at all. I explained the severity of the problem and advised that immediate emergency surgery was required to remove both her ovaries and uterus. The owner nodded in agreement. Before admitting the pet for surgery, I asked if there were any other questions, "Yes, but why does she have pus coming from her bladder?"

A dog's or cat's female urogenital system is somewhat like a modern plumbing fixture. Though a faucet may have only one knob, depending on how you adjust the valve, you can wash your hands with either very cold or very hot water, or somewhere in between. One external opening, the spigot, two separate water lines feeding into the fixture. The female dog's urogenital system shares a common opening, the vaginal vestibule, which can make discharge coming from the vagina difficult for an owner to determine if it is from the urinary or reproductive systems. A pyometra is a potentially life-threatening disease. It can theoretically happen to any female dog or cat that is not spayed, but it is most commonly seen in older female dogs. Why the uterus becomes infected is a matter of debate. It has been theorized that repeated exposure of the uterus to the hormonal changes of the reproductive cycle primes the uterus for this condition. The situation typically occurs four to eight weeks after the end of an estrous cycle. The cervix of the dog may or may not be open. If it is open, a pet owner will often notice a fetid, creamy white discharge.

More often than not, the cervix is closed. This allows the purulent material to build up within the uterus undetected. It is possible for the uterus to rupture, spilling the diseased uterine contents into the abdominal cavity. A pet owner may mistake the initial signs of a pyometra for a simple upset stomach, with evidence of lethargy, lack of appetite, vomiting and diarrhea. The best way to prevent this disease from occurring is to have a pet spayed early in its reproductive life.

PET OWNER: *Is the bit of skin hanging down between my cat's back legs her uterus?*

REPLY: I'm sorry to tell you this, but that bulge has nothing to do with a reproductive organ. It's a potbelly. Cats and dogs, males and females alike, can all suffer from obesity due to an overabundance of calories that robs our loved ones of their svelte figures. These chunky pets simply need to step away from the food bowl. A recent veterinary medical journal reported the first-ever liposuction surgery on an obese Chihuahua, but this is not the best way for the average full-figured pet to shed those extra pounds. If you can't tell if your pet is overweight, see your veterinarian. If there's a problem, he or she can help devise a weight-reduction diet that will result in a healthy weight loss.

A NEW CLIENT COMES INTO THE OFFICE WITH A TWELVE-YEAR-OLD longhaired cat. The cat's name is Fred. As I examine the cat, I realize that Fred is a female. In a state of utter disbelief, the owner asks, "Are you sure?"

It is common for someone to adopt a neutered stray and not know what the cat's or dog's sexual identity is. Few folks spend time examining a pet's privates, even though it's a pretty straightforward assessment. For a dog, just check between the legs; if the dog has a sheath attached to the belly, the dog is a boy.

Feline physiques can be a bit trickier—add a fluff of fur to a fuzzy derriere and all the pertinent anatomical landmarks are obliterated. Determining the sexual identity in kittens can be very difficult because their "parts" are all pretty small. If in doubt of your cat's chromosomal character, remember these simple rules of punctuation: if there's a colon down there, he's a male; a semicolon, she's female. Raise your puss's tail and if you spy two dots (one is the rectum, the other the opening that sheaths the penis), say hello to your new fella. If you view a dot (the rectum) and a slit below (the vagina) your Fred is really a Fredericka.

PET OWNER: *Isn't he cute? He only has one testicle, like his dad!*

REPLY: This dog is considered to be monorchid, which means he has only one testicle, and the condition is a subset of a disorder known as cryptorchid. The normal development for puppies or kittens is that both testes will be in the scrotum at ten days of age. During development in the mother's uterus, testes and ovaries originate from the same precursor tissue, located in the abdomen. The presence of the X or Y chromosome will determine if this primordial gonad will impart male or female characteristics. If the chromosomes determine that the puppy or kitten is going to be a male, the testes will travel through the inguinal canal in the groin and out to the scrotum. But not all species have testes in the scrotum year round. Male rabbits, for instance, will suck their balls into their bellies when it is not breeding season.

Adult dogs and cats are designed to have both testicles in the scrotum. If they are retained in the abdomen or within the inguinal canal, the pet is considered to be a cryptorchid (cryptic means hidden, orchid means testes). A testicle that is retained in the abdominal cavity will not produce sperm, but it will still secrete testosterone. Abdominally retained testes are exposed to higher temperatures than those that are allowed to swing in the breeze in the scrotum. Cryptorchid pets should be neutered to decrease the chances of developing testicular cancer. They should not be used at stud because they will pass along this trait.

TO FURTHER DEMYSTIFY THE CORPOREAL CHARACTERISTICS OF DOGS and cats, the following diagrams identify some of the more common anatomical landmarks:

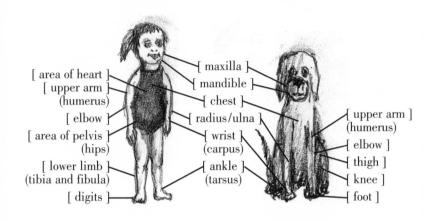

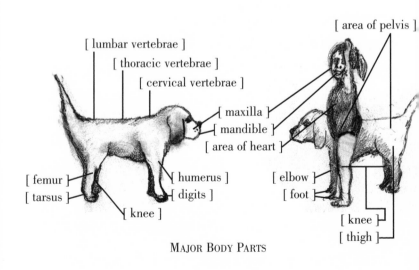

MAJOR BODY PARTS

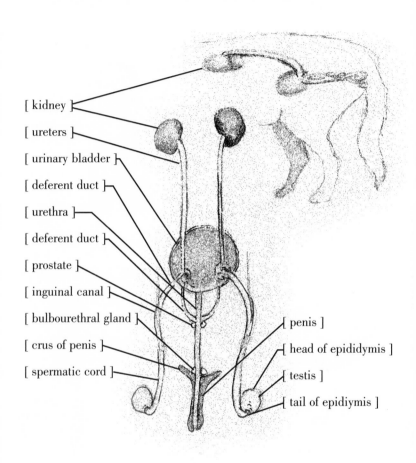

[kidney]

[ureters]

[urinary bladder]

[deferent duct]

[urethra]

[deferent duct]

[prostate]

[inguinal canal]

[bulbourethral gland]

[crus of penis]

[spermatic cord]

[penis]

[head of epididymis]

[testis]

[tail of epidiymis]

MALE CAT

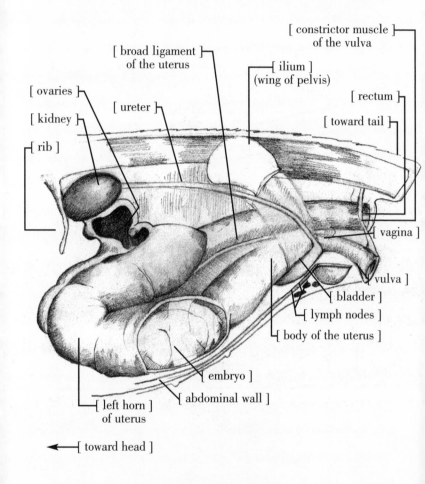

[constrictor muscle]
of the vulva

[broad ligament]
of the uterus

[ilium]
(wing of pelvis)

[rectum]

[ovaries]

[ureter]

[toward tail]

[kidney]

[rib]

[vagina]

[vulva]

[bladder]

[lymph nodes]

[body of the uterus]

[embryo]

[abdominal wall]

[left horn]
of uterus

[toward head]

FEMALE GENITAL SYSTEM
PREGNANT DOG OR CAT

124

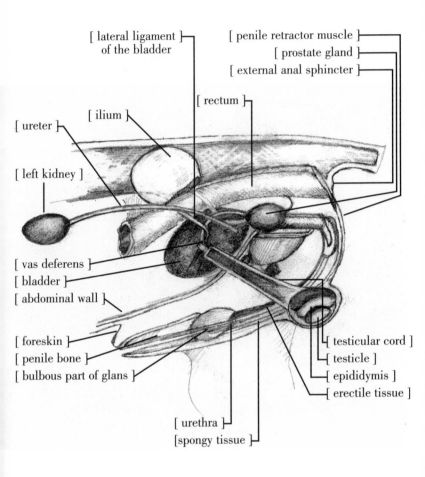

[lateral ligament]
of the bladder

[penile retractor muscle]

[prostate gland]

[external anal sphincter]

[rectum]

[ilium]

[ureter]

[left kidney]

[vas deferens]

[bladder]

[abdominal wall]

[foreskin]

[penile bone]

[bulbous part of glans]

[testicular cord]

[testicle]

[epididymis]

[erectile tissue]

[urethra]

[spongy tissue]

MALE DOG GENITAL SYSTEM

125

ACKNOWLEDGMENTS

Sex, when performed in a collaborative fashion is typically frowned upon. But this sex text was an unabashed joyous union of many—*minds*, that is. The dream of a book was given direction by Karen Perea and Greg Lee. Paddy Calistro and Scott McAuley of Angel City Press believed in an unpublished author and made this project a reality. Andrea Richards did a marvelous job editing and kept the "sarchasm" (the gulf between the author of sarcastic wit and the people who don't get it) in my work to a minimum. Stuart Rapeport added whimsy with his engaging illustrations. Graphic designer Amy Inouye of Future Studio married all the elements of word and art to give birth to this volume. And dear Chuck Morrell, my emissary to the literary world, thank you for spreading this sex-twisted ditty far and wide. My deepest heartfelt gratitude to all of you for your guidance, words of wisdom and friendship.

I am indebted to all my veterinary colleagues throughout the United States for sharing their stories with me. And I am grateful to all the dog and cat owners who cared enough about their furry charges to ask those occasionally perplexing questions. Finally, I offer very special thanks to all those very special pets who have left their paw prints of love on our hearts.

BERNADINE CRUZ, DVM

ANGEL CITY PRESS